SIX POETS OF THE
SAN FRANCISCO RENAISSANCE

Six Poets of the
San Francisco Renaissance

PORTRAITS AND CHECKLISTS

by David Kherdian

INTRODUCTION BY WILLIAM SAROYAN

THE GILIGIA PRESS • FRESNO

ALSO BY DAVID KHERDIAN

A Bibliography of William Saroyan: 1934-1964

Copyright © 1965, 1966, 1967 by David Kherdian
Library of Congress Catalog Card Number 67-24557
Printed at Anderson, Ritchie & Simon, Los Angeles, California
Design by Joseph Simon

To my mother and sister

Acknowledgment

I WOULD LIKE TO THANK each of the poets for their cooperation and assistance. In compiling the Michael McClure bibliography I was assisted through the use of Marshall Clements' catalog on the poet, which was then a work in progress. Without the use of the William Andrews Clark Memorial Library of the University of California, Los Angeles, and the Fresno State College Library archives, the Brother Antoninus bibliography could not have been written. The William Andrews Clark Memorial Library is an excellently staffed and sensitively run institution and is the library in this country I have most enjoyed visiting. The people of Fresno State College Library were especially helpful and friendly, and I am deeply grateful for their many courtesies. Individuals who made their libraries available were: Dave Haselwood, Al Krebs, Jr., Richard Duerden, Leland Meyerzov, and Robert Hawley. Libraries visited were the San Francisco Public Library, the rare book room of the University of California at Berkeley, and the Deering Library of Northwestern University. I would also like to thank each of the publishers for supplying needed information upon request. To all of these people and institutions my deepest thanks.

The Gary Snyder portrait was written from tape recorded conversations conducted in April, 1965. The Brother Antoninus interview was tape recorded March 1, 1966.

The excerpts from Philip Whalen's poetry are from his book, *Memoirs of an Interglacial Age.*

The photograph of Lawrence Ferlinghetti was taken in Paris by Annette Lena. The Sumi ink drawing of Brother Antoninus, and the paste-up drawing of David Meltzer are the work of Peter Le Blanc. The Brother Antoninus drawing is used through the courtesy of Mrs. Alix Geluardi. The photograph of Gary Snyder is by Don Allen. The Michael McClure collage is by Dorothy Hawley from photographs by Robert Hawley. The photograph of Philip Whalen is by Jay Blaise.

DAVID KHERDIAN

Contents

Introduction
by William Saroyan

A LOT OF THE WRITING going on these days, a lot of the
writing that's happening, as the writers themselves that I'm
thinking about might put it, a lot of the new writing that is
in fact new rather than for instance original or original-
looking, is often at first glance not writing at all, or at any
rate not writing as the habit of reading has come to expect
writing to be. But of course it is writing if for no better reason
than the reason that it is done with words. The thing that
seems to be back of it is a need for the writer to be himself
freely, which can be risky in the sense that most freely a
writer may discover that he is mainly a fool, or less, a nothing,
troubling terribly over it. Back of it is a need for the writer
to find out what has happened to the human race by finding
out what he himself is, after all of the time of the human race
right up to himself. Is this (absurdity or marvel, crook or
saint) what all the fuss was for? And of course the sensible
answer is, what else? But this thing that is back of this writing
along with the other things that are back of it, which may
finally be said to be unknown things or even unknowable
things, gives the writing its special peculiarity, or newness,
as if the whole business or reality of writing in the first place,
of the need and evolvement of it from communication by
means of vocal sounds, and finally speech, was being invented
all over again, even though the inventors did not know it, as
something put on paper for somebody to behold, or read. In
that dimension, this writing is least readily usable, and in a
sense most new, most difficult to relate to the rest of the body
of writing so far, and most of the time, or tentatively, most
easy to be impatient or even unkind about. Excellent writers
have found it possible to dismiss such writing, and the writers
of it, with a few dirty words in speech and a few ruthless
words in print, apparently failing to suspect for instance that
their own excellent writing is essentially as flawed and use-
less, excepting only insofar as it is easy to read, or entertaining,
or nearest the reader's own peace and comfort, as when he
is ready to fall asleep. This new writing may be said to be
troubled-young and trying—the writer is trying, that is, and
what he has managed is trying, or difficult, for the traditional,

old, or comfortable reader, who might say, "I know he's trying for something, but I don't care for it."

That's a lot of the writing, but a year or two later, or suddenly ten years later, these new and trying writers are now writing excellently, and so there is a lot of *that* writing, too.

And then their old writing, their first writing, which perhaps hadn't seemed quite so excellent is suddenly seen to have been quite excellent, after all, and perhaps better than their improved writing, improved as it was, as it always is, mainly by the passing of time, and by the writer's own drawing nearer to stoppage, so to put it, which if nothing else is at least always predictable. No writer writes forever, not even in terms of his own life and the time that may be allotted to it. He works and tries it out—on friends, on himself—and is guided by what he learns from their reading of what he wrote, and from his reading of what he wrote, and then he stops, either to think, or to stop, period.

What it is all about is everybody's insignificance, at least in relation to the whole, everybody's uselessness and meaninglessness, which is an affront in that everybody is also endowed by birth, by nature itself, with a built-in and believable theory of significance limitless in its potential, and a similar usefulness and meaning. In short, everybody is simultaneously nothing and everything, what do you do about it?

You do your best, and making a mess of it and failing, or putting it all in order and succeeding, come to almost the same thing, in that something has happened, somebody has been somewhere, writing of one kind or another has been written and has been read.

It is always all about the human race, about the fable and fantasy of it, and the race is probably too much for itself, excepting in the safest boundaries of religion and art, but even there the race is not too much for itself only in one man at a time, not in all of them together, where the evidence points unmistakably to the same order of helplessness that is in animals, fish, insects, microbes, and bacteria.

David Kherdian is interested in all of this, and in these papers about six poets of San Francisco he writes about all of this by writing simple and sensible and real things about the poets themselves, in their living reality, where they are, where they try, and about the writing these poets have done. His writing is so good that without knowing the poetry itself of the poets, I am made to feel glad that they are there, and to

believe in the unread and to me unknown poetry, which I
am sure I shall in time read and know. The whole nation
has gone on a half-official culture binge which isn't necessarily
spurious, but is definitely dangerous in that it can belittle
the unavoidable aloofness and separateness of the fixed poet,
and put into a kind of mirthless mob all of the fun and fight
and foolishness of the unfixed, the still trying, poet. From
having read David Kherdian on them, I like these poets very
much, and I like the ten times more of them I don't even
know about.

San Francisco, California
November 23, 1966

LAWRENCE FERLINGHETTI

Lawrence Ferlinghetti

"DOG" IS HOMER, a black and white mottled ball of fur of monstrous size and gentle disposition who pads quietly along after his master and best friend, Lawrence Ferlinghetti. His lineage is unknown and his origin indeterminate. His master says the front end is collie, the chassis mid-European schnauzer, and the rear end shepherd; but even to the scientific such distinctions must seem more amusing than accurate, for if Homer is made of such disparate parts than he seems to have taken the blend well and doesn't look pieced at all —just highly individual. His bark is so unauthoritative that it doesn't seem to be what he is saying at all, and running down the street in play with the neighborhood children, barking *Woof, Woof,* he looks more like a bear being a clown played by man than a lugubrious dog immortalized in verse.

The Ferlinghettis reside in an old terra-cotta Victorian house atop Portrero Hill that was restored, and escaped the demolition hammer, through funds from Lawrence Ferlinghetti's mother-in-law. That was 1954. The house was in shambles, Homer was residing at the S.P.C.A., and Ferlinghetti was a newly married unpublished writer. The following years were fruitful and productive, and there is now a successful book business and press, a number of books that have made his fame, and two healthy children, Julie, 5, and Lorenzo, 3.

Ferlinghetti does his writing in what looks and feels like an attic but is really nothing more than the upstairs half of their Victorian house. It has a small porch and a sizable window that looks out over the bay. Two large tables fit snugly into the corner of the room. The one paralleling the wall faces the window and is used to house the files and correspondence of City Lights authors. The chair is swivel, and the typewriter on which Ferlinghetti composes is on another desk that sits adjacent to the window. After he has begun his work Homer pads slowly up the stairs, walks into the open room and settles himself in the corner at the point at which the two tables converge to form an L. He lies here quietly asleep, half-asleep, or wide-awake. If spoken to he looks up quietly and lies back down. On a normal day man and dog are the followers of this routine from eight in the morning until noon. If the day is going to be warm the attic-like quarters are the first place to feel the heat, and on winter days there is a pot-bellied stove to keep things at a working temperature.

Ferlinghetti, now 47 and sporting a closely cropped salt and pepper beard, is tall and lean, and takes the long silent strides of a much younger man. Like his verse, his speech is laconic, but for reasons opposite of his writing. His speech comes from a mind that seems intentionally halved: one being the banal words he speaks, the other the thoughtful words he considers. The cool distance he keeps from outsiders makes him seem phlegmatic, even churlish, and to the observer across the room he seems dull in outline, his eyes like two opaque Mexican beads; but close up, and seen when his eyes are looking at something observed, they look more like the hard blue eyes of a gunner's mate. It's as if he'd willed all his energy to be mental, but without changing the look of impenetrable innocence and inscrutability on his face, or without even becoming cerebral—but thoughtful, observant, concerned with the minutest detail;—finding in such minutiae a universal disposition.

Around one o'clock of a normal day Ferlinghetti says goodbye to his family, gets in his black Volkswagen, and heads for his bookstore in North Beach. Originally named City Lights Pocket Bookshop by Ferlinghetti and his partner, Peter Martin, the store has since taken on a modified name: City Lights Books, and a new partner: Shigeyoshi Murao. It is a unique, distinctive, and original bookstore for several reasons. First advertised as the first all paperback bookstore in America, it has since taken on claims that may not be for national boasting, but to an ever growing segment of the population it has become a Mecca, and more, to the transient and local Bohemian, who have made of it a home, a meeting place, and a stomping ground. In addition to being among like-souls, the Bohemian has come to find most specifically in this store, and in the North Beach section generally, a sanctuary from the bourgeois society he has escaped.

City Lights has become the focal point of this rebellion.

The store consists of three levels. At street level the entrance, where a clerk sits in a cubicle in the center of what can only be called a "tiny" room. The upstairs, which is reached by a curving inside stair that is so narrow it has to be half crawled, contains all of the store's foreign language paperbacks. The downstairs is a converted basement, an area

4

perhaps three or four times as large as the combined two floors above, and contains the store's offices; one of the closed-off makeshift rooms being Ferlinghetti's. At the head of the basement stairs is perhaps the world's most unique bulletin board. In code, in a variety of vernaculars, in verse, and occasionally in plain English, are requests for a rider or riders to New York, models of various description and purpose, lovers of both sex for either or both, and even messages from middle-aged Chinese and American landladies wanting to rent rooms and apartments. Also: posters, petitions, announcements, descriptions of someone someone else is looking for, or someone who has heard someone they once met somewhere else is in town whom they'd like to reach, but they only know their first name and little else—

> Paul, Allen's friend
> We met in Buffalo last summer,
> heard you fell in last week—
> blow this number: 396-2478.
> (signed) Phil
> Jean
> Pat

And above the bulletin board, open mail boxes holding letters and notes for those who are coming into town or are passing through. Downstairs, in addition to the inevitable books, are further messages to the people, but in more controlled forms. On the wall a revolving commercial and artistic venture: the watercolors of Kenneth Patchen; photographs by Jim Hatch of the principals of last year's poetry conference in Berkeley; one man shows of painters and photographers of recent vintage, as a rule depicting jazz and psychedelic experiences; and also, at the moment, a printed broadside of Allen Ginsberg, standing naked with Tibetan finger cymbals in his hands and framed in his own phallic in a drawing by Robert LaVigne; a fight poster by Michael McClure with photos of the opponents: Billy the Kid and Jean Harlow; another printed poster of McClure, naked, in beast make-up, titled: *Poetry Is a Muscular Principle;* and Philip Whalen's poem in broadside, *The Goddess.* In the rear of the basement a rack containing books in *The Pocket Poets Series,* and in back of that a horse-shoe cubicle containing the literature of the Beat Generation. On the swinging door that houses the store's office space, the jocular warning: *Beware of Dog,* and an announcement: *Gone*

5

Fishing. Hanging above the door, an empty bird cage with an inserted sign that reads: *No Trespassing.*

The publishing history of City Lights Books is as old as the store itself, beginning with the now defunct *City Lights* magazine, which pre-dated the store but helped name it, and moving on to the now famous *The Pocket Poets Series,* which began with Ferlinghetti's own book, *Pictures of the Gone World,* and then next published Allen Ginsberg's *Howl and Other Poems,* which immediately made the series, the store, the Beat Generation, and poetry in America famous, by winning a trial suit against a charge that the book was obscene. The press's most recent venture is the *City Lights Journal,* which is published annually and is now in its third year.

Around four o'clock, his day completed, Ferlinghetti returns home. When he drives up in front of his house Homer, who has been sitting on the front porch waiting, slowly descends the stairs, pads up to his friend and barks. The face looking down at him whispers something not for ears to hear and they turn and begin walking up the stairs.

The sign in the window says: *Make Love Not War.*

6

TITLE PAGES, NOS. 12 AND 7

BOOKS, BROADSIDES & TRANSLATIONS

1. Ruskin's Turner, Child of Light, by Lawrence Ferling[1] n.p. [New York, N.Y.], Columbia University, 1948.

   Typescript. Master's thesis. Submitted in partial fulfillment of the requirements for the degree of Master of Arts, Faculty of Philosophy, Columbia University. 3 copies only. Two copies on deposit at Columbia University, the third in the possession of the author.

2. La Cité Symbole Dans la Poésie Moderne de Langue Anglaise (À la Recherche D'une Tradition Metropolitaine), by Lawrence Ferling, M.A., 1950.

   Typescript. Principal thesis for Doctorate for the University of Paris. It received Very Honorable Mention (Mention Tres Honorable). 4 copies only. Two copies reside at the University of Paris (Sorbonne), one copy with Raymond Lasbergnas, who was Ferlinghetti's professor, and one copy with Lawrence Ferlinghetti.

3a. Pictures of the Gone World. San Francisco, Calif., The City Lights Pocket Bookshop (The Pocket Poets Series Number One), November, 1955.

   Stiff black wrappers, with yellow title label hand-pasted and extending to both sides. The first edition may be identified by the absence of such notification, and by the separate title label, pasted over, as noted above. About 500 copies only for the first edition. All reprints carry such notice on the back cover. The second printing, called "Second Edition," is in variant white wrappers. The biographical notice and blurb on the back cover were changed for later printings.[2] This book is presently in the 10th printing, with 38,455 copies having been printed to date.

3b. 25 copies bound in black cloth over boards with the title label from the paper-bound issue pasted on the front cover.

[1]In 1954 the poet restored the original family name which had been shortened by his father.

[2]All City Lights publications with the exception of *Antonin Artaud, Anthology*, edited by Jack Hirschman, and *A Little Anthology of Surrealist Poetry*, edited by Jean-Jacques Lebel, are edited by Lawrence Ferlinghetti, who has also written all blurbs for his press (including those for his own books) with the exception of the blurb for, *William S. Burroughs & Allen Ginsberg, The Yage Letters*, which was written by Allen Ginsberg.

4. TENTATIVE DESCRIPTION OF A DINNER GIVEN TO PRO-
MOTE THE IMPEACHMENT OF PRESIDENT EISENHOWER.
San Francisco, Calif., Golden Mountain Press, May, 1958.

White printed self-wrappers. The publisher's device is in gold for
the first edition, and is thereafter printed in black. About 1000
copies were printed for the first edition. There were either 5 or 6
printings totaling about 17,500 copies.

5. A CONEY ISLAND OF THE MIND. Norfolk, Connecticut, A
New Directions Book, May, 1958.

Pictorial wrappers. Cover photograph by The Bettman Archive. The
first edition may be identified by the absence of such notification on
the copyright page. Subsequent printings carry the printing notice
on the copyright page and on the back cover. The photo of the poet
on the back cover was changed between the 10th and 11th printings.
There were 3887 copies printed for the first edition. It is presently
in the 14th printing, with 162,445 copies printed to date.

6a. SELECTIONS FROM PAROLES BY JACQUES PRÉVERT. San
Francisco, Calif., City Lights Books (The Pocket Poets
Series: Number 9), December, 1958.

Black and white printed wrappers. Translated by Ferlinghetti and
containing his "Translator's Note" on pp. 3-6. There were 1500 copies
printed for the first edition. 7542 copies have been printed to date.

6b. *Selections from 'Paroles'.* Penguin Modern European Poets Series,
No. D84. Middlesex, England, 1965. Contains a revised "Translator's
Note" by Ferlinghetti.

6c. 4th printing (City Lights). Revised "Translator's Note" as above.

7a. HER. Norfolk, Connecticut, A New Directions Book, November, 1960.

Yellow cloth over boards in the dust jacket. The cover drawing is by
the author. 1500 copies only. This is Ferlinghetti's only published
novel.

7b. Paperback edition from same plates with dust jacket design from
clothbound edition serving as front cover illustration. 6500 copies in
first edition printing. Now in 7th printing in a total of 33,342 copies.

ERRATA: The following changes were made for the 4th and all subsequent printings: half-title for quote, p. 7; *O god,* last two words,
last line, dropped, p. 157; blank for biographical notice, p. 158; new
list for old, pp. 159-160.

8. ONE THOUSAND FEARFUL WORDS FOR FIDEL CASTRO. San
Francisco, Calif., A City Lights Publication, January,
1961.

Folded broadside. The first edition may be identified by the absence
of such notification. The second printing is so stated on the back
cover. The first edition consisted of 2000 copies; the second printing
of 3000 copies.

9. BERLIN. San Francisco, Calif., Golden Mountain Press, October, 1961.

> White printed self-wrappers. 1000 copies printed for the first edition. Number of copies printed for the second printing is not known. There were two printings only.

10a. STARTING FROM SAN FRANCISCO. Norfolk, Connecticut, A New Directions Book, December, 1961.

> Pictorial paper over boards. Cover photograph of Machu Picchu by Cornell Capa. Cover design by Gilda Kuhlman. A 33-1/3 r.p.m. record is inserted in a jacket on the rear end paper and contains readings from the book by the poet. The first edition consisted of 7430 copies.

10b. Second binding. 5,070 copies from unbound sheets remaining from the first printing were bound in the fall of 1966 in pictorial wrappers, with the same photograph being used that served for the front cover illustration of the first edition, but without the phonograph record.

11. THOUGHTS OF A CONCERTO OF TELEMAN. San Francisco, Calif., [The Four Seasons Foundation], October, 1963.

> Broadside. Illustrated by Eleanor Dickinson. A series of eight broadsides by as many poets in conjunction with the San Francisco Arts Festival. Issued in portfolio with a title label for the set on the front cover. 300 copies, of which 250 were placed for sale. Printed by East Wind Printers.

12. UNFAIR ARGUMENTS WITH EXISTENCE: Seven Plays for a New Theatre. New York, N.Y., A New Directions Paperbook, December, 1963.

> Pictorial wrappers. Title page drawing adapted from Cuban theatre poster by Ferlinghetti. The first edition may be noted by the absence of such notification. The second printing is so stated on the back cover. The first edition consisted of 8,988 copies. It is presently in the second printing with 19,050 copies printed to date.

> ERRATA: *by New Directions Publishing Corporation*, inserted page iv, after line 17; *(Shooky begins to move.)* for *(Shooky does not move.)*, page 63, lines 3-4; photo of Tom Rosqui appears on p. 49, having been erroneously omitted from the first edition; *Revolution happen now!*, added to page 63, line 15, with the stage direction following dropped; *still holding him back*, stage direction added, page 63, line 16; *Oh, babee! Don't leave me! How'll we manage without you!* for *They, they told us they'd—*, page 63, lines 16-17; *Oh, sweetie—*for *they're—*, page 63, line 18; *I give up!* added to page 63, line 30; *Yes—please. I give up—I do, I do—I see now— yes, I do—It's not too late—*added to page 63, last line, and page 64, lines 1-2; *too late—*added to page 64, line 17; *too late—too late!* added to page 64, lines 19-20; italicized stage directions added to the play, *The Customs Collector in Baggy Pants*, pp. 107-113.

13. ROUTINES. New York, N.Y.. A New Directions Paperbook, December, 1964.

> White decorative wrappers. Cover drawing by Roland Topor from
> a design by the author. The first edition consisted of 8300 copies. It
> is presently in the second printing with 16,466 copies printed to date.
> ERRATUM: *a slip—into eternity—for a sleep—*, page 5, line 16.

14. WHERE IS VIETNAM? n.p. [San Francisco, Calif.], City
Lights Books, August, 1965.

> Folded broadside. The second printing may be identified by its desig-
> nation beneath the poem. The first edition consisted of 1000 copies,
> with 2000 copies printed for the second printing.

15. TO FUCK IS TO LOVE AGAIN; *Kyrie Eleison Kerista,* or,
The Situation in the West, Followed by a Holy Proposal.
New York, N.Y., Fuck You Press, 1965.

> Stapled wrappers; text and covers mimeographed. 1000 copies only.

FILMS

16. HAVE YOU SOLD YOUR DOZEN ROSES?

> 9 minutes. 16mm film, in black and white. Produced by Philip
> Greene, David Meyers, and Allen Willis at the California School of
> Fine Arts Film Workshop in 1957. The narration was composed
> spontaneously by Ferlinghetti as a free verse poem paced to the
> images of the film. This film was accepted for showing at the Edin-
> burgh International Film Festival of 1957, and has been shown in
> many countries of Europe and museums in California. A script for
> the film was not made; the only written script in existence being a
> hand written copy made by the poet and in his possession.

FUGITIVE PIECES & EPHEMERA

17. LAWRENCE FERLINGHETTI. n.p. [Spoleto, Italy], [Spoleto
Festival], n.d. [June, 1965].

> 14 pp. mimeographed sheaf of poems, 13 x 8-11/16 inches. Untitled
> except for poet's name at top of page. Two editions of about 200
> copies each were made in English and Italian. Poems contained:
> "Berlin," "Big Fat Hairy Vision," "The Man Who Rode Away,"
> "In Goya's Greatest Scenes," "Sometime During Eternity," "Dog,"
> and "Underwear."

18. CHRIST CLIMBED DOWN. n.p. [New York, N.Y.], Syracuse
University, December 16, 1965.

> Folded broadside, 11-5/16 x 4-2/8 inches. The poem is printed on
> the front cover, the inside covers blank, with colophon on back cover.

FOREIGN EDITIONS

19. POEMA PARA PROMOVER EL ENJUICIAMIENTO DEL PRESI-
DENTE EISENHOWER POR EL POETA NORTEAMERICANO.
n.p. [Buenos Aires, Argentina], [Agua Viva, Edicion
Especial], n.d. [1959?].

> Folded broadside. This is a pirated edition.

12

20. DESCRIPTION TENTATIVA DE UNA OFRECIDA PARA PRO-
MOVER EL "IMPEACHMENT" DEL PRESIDENTE EISEN-
HOWER, por Laurense [SIC] Ferlinghetti. n.p. [San Juan,
Puerto Rico], n.d. [1959?].

Printed self-wrappers. Translated by René Jiménez Malaret. This
is a pirated edition.

21. A CONEY ISLAND OF THE MIND. London, England,
Hutchinson & Co. Ltd., 1959.

Decorative paper over boards, cloth backed spine. The dust jacket
contains a photograph of the author.

22. LA QUATRIEME PERSONNE DU SINGULIER. Paris, France,
Julliard (Les Lettres Nouvelles 18), 1961.

Printed wrappers. Translated by Jacqueline Bernard. Drawing of
Ferlinghetti by Monique Métrot. English title: Her.

23. EIN CONEY ISLAND DES INNEREN KARUSSELLS. Weisbaden, Germany, Limes Verlag, 1962.

Pictorial wrappers. Translated by Erika Gutermann.

24. LUNA PARK VHLAVE. Prague, Czechoslovakia, Statni
Nakladatelstvi Krásné Literatury a Umeni, 1962.

Printed wrappers. Translated by Jan Zábrana. Frontispiece photo
of Ferlinghetti.

25. SIE. Weisbaden, Germany, Limes Verlag, 1963.

Yellow cloth with the dust jacket identical with the first edition dust
jacket of Her. Translated by Walter Schmiele.

26. DESCRIPTION EXPERIMENTAL DE UNA CENA DADA PARA
PROMOVER EL ENJUICIAMIENTO DEL PRESIDENTE EISEN-
HOWER. Mexico City, Mexico, August-September, 1963.

Broadside. Illustrated by Arnold Belkin.

27. STARTING ZE SAN FRANCISCA. Prague, Czechoslovakia,
Mladá Fronta, 1964.

Decorative white cloth in the dust jacket. Translated by Vojtech
Mihálik and Ján Vilikovsky.

28. SMUTNA NAHA JAZDKYNA. Bratislava, Czechoslovakia,
Slovensky Spisovatel, 1965.

White decorative cloth over boards. Text and cover illustrations by
Frantisek Kudlac. Translated by Vojtech Mihálik and Ján Vilikovsky. A photograph and a note on the author appear at the back of
the book. Issued with a slip case. Composed of the two titles: A Coney
Island of the Mind and Starting from San Francisco.

29. HUN. Fredensborg, Denmark, Arena, 1965.

Decorative wrappers, with illustrations same as first edition dust
jacket. Translated by Erik Thygesen.

13

PERIODICAL AND NEWSPAPER CONTRIBUTIONS

[*All contributions are poems, or translations of poems, unless otherwise noted. This section is divided into two parts. This first part contains contributions by Lawrence Ferling. Note: All contributions to the San Francisco Chronicle are book reviews. None of this material was ever reprinted. Each review appears in the This World section of the newspaper, which is a Sunday supplement. This information is given in the first entry and is not repeated. All contributions to Counterpoint and Arts Digest magazines are articles and were never reprinted.*]

30. San Francisco Chronicle, This World, Sunday, July 22, 1951.
"Six of the Recent Poetry Books."

31. San Francisco Chronicle, September 23, 1951.
"A New Look at Two Poets of the 16th Century."

32. San Francisco Chronicle, September 30, 1951.
Poems in Process, by Phyllis Bartlett.

33. San Francisco Chronicle, October 7, 1951.
The Autobiogrpahy of William Carlos Williams.

34. San Francisco Chronicle, November 18, 1951.
"Nine New Volumes of Poetry."

35. San Francisco Chronicle, November 25, 1951.
The Collected Poems of W. B. Yeats and *Selected Writings* by Paul Eluard.

36. San Francisco Chronicle, December 2, 1951.
Auden: An Introductory Essay, by Richard Haggart.

37. San Francisco Chronicle, December 9, 1951.
The Course Is Upward, by George Scarbrough.

38. Counterpoint: The Magazine of Music and Allied Arts, Vol. XVII, No. 1. San Francisco, Calif., Stanley Associates, January, 1952.
Managing Editor: Donald Dudley. Contains the article, "Expressionism in San Francisco Painting Today."

39. San Francisco Chronicle, January 6, 1952.
"Some New Additions to the Poetry Shelf."

40. San Francisco Chronicle, January 13, 1952.
Stephan Mallarme· Poems, translated by Roger Fry.

41. San Francisco Chronicle, January 20, 1952.
Praise to the End!, by Theodore Roethke.

42. San Francisco Chronicle, January 27, 1952.
Winged Chariot and Other Poems, by Walter de la Mare.

43. San Francisco Chronicle, February 3, 1952.
"The Poetry Shelf."

44. San Francisco Chronicle, February 17, 1952.
A Mother Goes to War, by Helen Jones.

45. San Francisco Chronicle, March 9, 1952.
"Dylan Thomas and Other Poets."

46. San Francisco Chronicle, April 6, 1952.
The Life of the Virgin Mary, by Rainer Maria Rilke, translated by Stephen Spender.

47. San Francisco Chronicle, April 13, 1952.
Chivers' Life of Poe, edited by Richard Beale Davis.

48. San Francisco Chronicle, April 20, 1952.
A Little Treasury of Modern Poetry, edited by Oscar Williams.

49. San Francisco Chronicle, April 27, 1952.
The Complete Poetry and Selected Prose of John Donne, edited by Charles M. Coffin.

50. Inferno, Nos. 6 & 7. San Francisco, Calif., Inferno, May, 1952.
Edited by Leslie Hedley. Contains "Brother, Brother" by the poet and his translations of 8 poems by Jacques Prévert, "La Belle Saison," "Pater Noster," "Quartier Libre," "Lament of Vincent," "The Discourse on Peace," "Song," "To Paint the Portrait of a Bird," and *"Chris Bjerkness: 2 poems* 1. Spring Night, 2. The Dead Foal."

51. Counterpoint: The Magazine of Music and Allied Arts, Vol. XVII, No. 5. San Francisco, Calif., Stanley Associates, May, 1952.
Edited by Donald Dudley. Contains the article, "The Labaudt Gallery: A Proving Ground for Tomorrow's Artists."

52. San Francisco Chronicle, May 4, 1952.
Waters Over Linn Creek Town, by Ralph Alan McCanse; *The Frenzied Poets, Andrey Biely and the Russian Symbolists*, by Oleg A. Maslenikov; and *Modern American Poetry*, edited by B. Rajan.

53. San Francisco Chronicle, May 11, 1952.
Four Men West and Other Poems, by Jennette Yeatman.

54. San Francisco Chronicle, May 18, 1952.

The Background of Modern Poetry, by J. Isaacs.

55. San Francisco Chronicle, May 25, 1952.

Poems of John Keats, edited by John Middleton Murry; *Ezra Pound and the Cantos*, by Harold H. Watts; and *The Enchanted Grindstone*, by Henry Morton Robinson.

56. Counterpoint: The Magazine of Music and Allied Arts, Vol. XVII, No. 6. San Francisco, Calif., June, 1952.

Edited by Donald Dudley. Contains the article, "Side View of a Poet," an article concerning a reading given by Dylan Thomas in San Francisco.

57. San Francisco Chronicle, June 15, 1952.

The Suburb by the Sea, by Robert Hillyer.

58. San Francisco Chronicle, June 22, 1952.

Modern Poetry and the Christian Tradition: A Study in the Relation of Christianity to Culture, by Amos N. Wilder.

59. San Francisco Chronicle, July 6, 1952.

"Three Poets in Retrospect—and Reviews of Contemporary Verse."

60. San Francisco Chronicle, August 3, 1952.

New and Selected Poems, by Thomas Hornsby Ferril.

61. San Francisco Chronicle, August 24, 1952.

Firebird: A Study of D. H. Lawrence, by Dallas Kenmore, and *Poetry in Our Time*, by Babette Deutsch.

62. San Francisco Chronicle, August 31, 1952.

The Stubborn Root, by Joel Keith.

63. San Francisco Chronicle, September 7, 1952.

"Short Reviews of Some of the Recent Poetry Books."

64. San Francisco Chronicle, September 14, 1952.

Mild Silver and Furious Gold, by Vesta Nickerson.

65. San Francisco Chronicle, October 12, 1952.

Poems, by Ridgely Torrence.

66. San Francisco Chronicle, October 19, 1952.

On Reading Poetry, by Aubrey de Selincourt.

67. San Francisco Chronicle, October 26, 1952.

Poems, by Robert Simeon Adams.

68. San Francisco Chronicle, November 9, 1952.

Rhymes of a Rebel, by Robert Service; *Elizabethan Poetry: A Study of Conventions, Meanings and Expression*; and *The First Morning*, by Peter Viereck.

69. San Francisco Chronicle, November 23, 1952.

Blade, by Candace Thurber; *A Book of Beauty: An Anthology of Words and Pictures*, by John Hadfield; and *Kentucky Is My Land*, by Jesse Stuart.

70. Counterpoint. San Francisco, Calif., Stanley Associates, December, 1952.

Edited by Donald Dudley. Contains "In the Hush of Concrete," an article about a reading by Kenneth Patchen.

71. San Francisco Chronicle, December 7, 1952.

Sonnets for Eve and Other Poems, by Clara Aiken Speer.

72. San Francisco Chronicle, December 14, 1952.

The Complete Poems and Plays, by T. S. Eliot.

73. Goad, Vol. 2, No. 1., Sausalito, Calif., Horace Schwartz, January, 1953.

Contains "Alicante," "The Eclipse," "First Day," and "And the Fete Continues," by Jacques Prévert, translated by Laurence Ferling.

74. San Francisco Chronicle, January 11, 1953.

"Some of the New Poetry Books."

75. San Francisco Chronicle, January 18, 1953.

The Dragon and the Unicorn, by Kenneth Rexroth, and "Some of the Recent Poetry Books."

76. San Francisco Chronicle, January 25, 1953.

The Poet of the Iliad, by H. T. Wade-Gery, and *Walt Whitman, Thinker and Artist*, by Arthur E. Briggs.

77. San Francisco Chronicle, February 1, 1953.

So Many Daughters, by Edna Lou Walton.

78. San Francisco Chronicle, March 1, 1953.

Poems, by Miguel de Unamuno.

79. San Francisco Chronicle, March 8, 1953.

Paths of Yesterday, by Fay Jackson, and *With All My Love*, by Frank Kimball.

80. Art Digest: The News Magazine of Art, Vol. 27, No. 14. New York, N.Y., Art Digest, Inc., April 15, 1953.

Edited by Belle Krasne. Contains the articles, "Muralist Refregier and the Haunted Post Office," and "San Francisco." Lawrence Ferling began this issue as the continuing San Francisco correspondent.

81. San Francisco Chronicle, April 5, 1953.

The Fourth King, by LeRoy Smith, and *The Written Word*, by Carleton Drewry.

17

82. San Francisco Chronicle, April 12, 1953.
"The Works of Dylan Thomas and Other Poets."

83. San Francisco Chronicle, April 19, 1953.
The Bat Brothers, by Frank Borden Hanes.

84. San Francisco Chronicle, April 26, 1953.
Twentieth-Century German Verse: A Selection, translated by Herman Salinger.

85. San Francisco Chronicle, May 3, 1953.
Hoelderin: His Poems, by Michael Hamburger.

86. San Francisco Chronicle, May 10, 1953.
Selected Poems of Claude McKay, and *The Eternal Variant: Love Songs and Lyrics*, by Edna Walker-Malcosky.

87. Art Digest: The News Magazine of Art, Vol. 27, No. 16. New York, N.Y., Art Digest, Inc., May 15, 1953.
Edited by Belle Krasne. Contains the article, "San Francisco."

88. San Francisco Chronicle, May 17, 1953.
"Some Recent Books of Poetry."

89. City Lights, Number Three. San Francisco, Calif., City Lights, Spring, 1953.
Edited by Peter Martin, Norma Bowkett, Wilder Bentley, Herbert Kauffman, Joseph Kostolefsky, and Charles Polk. Contains translations from Jacques Prévert's *Paroles*, "The Dunce," "School of Fine Arts," "Autumn," "Breakfast," "Sunday," and "One Shouldn't."

90. San Francisco Chronicle, May 24, 1953.
Wordsworth and the Literature of Travel, by Charles Norton Coe.

91. Inferno, No. 9. San Francisco, Calif., Inferno Press, 1953.
Edited by Leslie Hedley. Contributing editor: Harry Hooton. Contains reproductions of two paintings: *Open City* and *The Balcony*.

92. Art Digest: The News Magazine of Art, Vol. 27, No. 17. New York, N.Y., Art Digest, Inc., June, 1953.
Edited by Belle Krasne. Contains the article, "San Francisco."

93. City Lights, Number 5. San Francisco, Calif., City Lights, 1953.
Edited by Peter Martin. Contains "A Wake for Thomas."

94. San Francisco Chronicle, July 19, 1953.
Winds, by St. John Perse.

18

95. Contact, Vol. 2, No. 3. Toronto, Canada, Contact Press, May-August, 1953.

Contains translations of four poems by Jacques Prévert, "Barbara," "Osiris, or the Flight in Egypt," "I've Seen Some of Them," and "Tamiliae."

96. San Francisco Chronicle, August 16, 1953.

Making a Poem: An Inquiry Into the Creative Process, by Melville Cane, and *The True Voice of Feeling: Studies in English Romantic Poetry*, by Herbert Read.

97. San Francisco Chronicle, August 23, 1953.

To Lighten My House, by Alastair Reid, and *The Finer Tone: Keat's Major Poems*, by Earl R. Wasserman.

98. San Francisco Chronicle, August 30, 1953.

Heir to Eden, by Margaret Lewis Albanese.

99. San Francisco Chronicle, September 13, 1953.

The Collected Plays of W. B. Yeats, and *The Gypsy Ballads of Federico Garcia Lorca*, translated by Rolfe Humphries.

100. San Francisco Chronicle, September 20, 1953.

"The 'Lost' Poetry of Scharmel Iris."

101. San Francisco Chronicle, October 4, 1953.

The Translations of Ezra Pound, and *Long Stems, Colored*, by Charlene Palmer.

102. Art Digest, Vol. 28, No. 2. New York, N.Y., Art Digest, Inc., October 15, 1953.

Edited by Belle Krasne. Contains the article, "San Francisco."

103. San Francisco Chronicle, October 18, 1953.

Dry Sun, Dry Wind, by David Wagoner, and *The Plane and the Shadow*, by Norman Rosten.

104. Arts Digest, Vol. 28, No. 4. Art Digest, Inc., November 15, 1953.

Edited by Belle Krasne. Contains the article, "San Francisco."

105. San Francisco Chronicle, November 22, 1953.

The Year One and Other Poems, by Kathleen Raine, and *The Poems of T'Ao Ch'Ien*, translated by Lily Pao-Hu and Marjorie Sinclair.

106. San Francisco Chronicle, November 29, 1953.

Poems 1940-1953, by Karl Shapiro, and *Collected Poems*, by Conrad Aiken, and *Hilaire Belloc: No Alienated Man*, by Frederick Wilhelmsen.

107. The California Quarterly, Vol. 2, No. 2. Los Angeles, Calif., The California Quarterly, Winter, 1953.

Edited by Sanora Babb, Leslie Edgely, Thomas McGrath, Wilma Shore, Lawrence P. Spingarn, and Phillip Stevenson. Contains translations by the poet of Jacques Prévert's "Promenade de Picasso," and "The Last Supper."

108. San Francisco Chronicle, January 10, 1954.

The Waking: Poems 1933-1953, by Theodore Roethke, and *Exile and Other Poems*, by St. John Perse, translated by Denis Devlin.

109. San Francisco Chronicle, January 17, 1954.

Wing Your Joy!, by Othelia Lilly, and "An Appraisal of 1953's Poetry."

110. San Francisco Chronicle, January 31, 1954.

"Additions to the Poetry Shelf."

111. San Francisco Chronicle, February 7, 1954.

The Art of Worldly Wisdom, by Kenneth Rexroth.

112. San Francisco Chronicle, February 21, 1954.

"The Lower Case 'i' of E. E. Cummings—And Other Poets."

113. San Francisco Chronicle, March 7, 1954.

The Cherubinic Wanderer, by Angelus Silesius.

114. San Francisco Chronicle, March 14, 1954.

"For Jeffers the Purpose of Poetry Is 'To Feel Greatly ...'"

115. Arts Digest, Vol. 28, No. 12. New York, N.Y., The Art Digest, Inc., March 15, 1954.

Managing editor: Hubert Crehan. Contains "San Francisco by Lawrence Ferling,/ 'Hour of Absinthe.'"

116. San Francisco Chronicle, March 21, 1954.

Sonnets and Verse, by Hilaire Belloc.

117. San Francisco Chronicle, April 25, 1954.

The Desert Music and Other Poems, by William Carlos Williams, and *Animal, Vegetable, Mineral*, by Babette Deutsch, and *Angel of Accidence: Poems*, by Peter Kane Dufault.

118. Art Digest, Vol. 28, No. 17. New York, N.Y., Art Digest Inc., June 1, 1954.

Managing editor: Hubert Crehan. Contains the article, "Dufy in America."

119. San Francisco Chronicle, June 6, 1954.

Selected Poems, 1946-1953, by Leslie Woolf Hedley.

20

120. San Francisco Chronicle, June 13, 1954.
"Reviews of Some of the New Books of Poetry."

121. San Francisco Chronicle, June 20, 1954.
In the Cold Country: Poems, by Barbara Howes.

122. San Francisco Chronicle, June 27, 1954.
John Keats: The Living Year, by Robert Gettings.

123. San Francisco Chronicle, July 18, 1954.
"Four New Books of Poetry by Women."

124. Arts Digest, Vol. 28, No. 19, New York, N.Y., Arts Digest, Inc., August 1, 1954.
Managing editor: Hubert Crehan. Contains the article, "San Francisco/Bay Area Roundup."

125. San Francisco Chronicle, August 8, 1954.
The Complete Poetry and Prose of Walt Whitman.

126. San Francisco Chronicle, September 26, 1954.
Libretto for the Republic of Liberia, by M. B. Tolson.

127. Arts Digest, Vol. 29, No. 1. New York, N.Y., The Art Digest, Inc., October 1, 1954.
Managing editor: Hubert Crehan. Contains the article, "San Francisco."

128. San Francisco Chronicle, October 3, 1954.
The Toy Fair, by Howard Moss.

129. San Francisco Chronicle, October 31, 1954.
The Metamorphoses of Ovid: An English Version, by A. E. Watts.

130. San Francisco Chronicle, November 28, 1954.
The Collected Poems, by Wallace Stevens, and *Poems: 1923-1954*, by E. E. Cummings.

131. San Francisco Chronicle, December 5, 1954.
The Famous Boating Party: And Other Poems in Prose, by Kenneth Patchen, and *The Major Poets: English and American*, edited by Charles M. Coffin.

132. San Francisco Chronicle, December 12, 1954.
Collected Poems, by James Stephens.

133. Arts Digest, Vol. 29, No. 6. New York, N.Y., Arts Digest, Inc., December 15, 1954.
Managing editor: Hubert Crehan. Contains the article, "San Francisco: Primitivism and Modern Art."

21

134. Arts Digest, Vol. 29, No. 8. New York, N.Y., Arts Digest, Inc., January 15, 1955.

Managing editor: Hubert Crehan. Contains the article, "San Francisco."

135. San Francisco Chronicle, January 16, 1955.

An Almanac for Amorists, by James Broughton.

136. Arts Digest, Vol. 29, No. 15. New York, N.Y., Arts Digest, Inc., May 1, 1955.

Edited by Jonathan Marshall. Contains the article, "San Francisco."

137. Arts Digest, Vol. 29, No. 19. New York, N.Y., Arts Digest, Inc., August 1, 1955.

Edited by Jonathan Marshall. Contains the article, "San Francisco." This is the last issue in which Ferlinghetti was the San Francisco correspondent.

138. The Miscellaneous Man, No. 10. Berkeley, Calif., William J. Margolis, January, 1957.

Edited by William J. Margolis. Contains poems nos. 5 and 6 from *Pictures of the Gone World*, and "Aphorisms and Other Fragments from the Poetry of Rene Char," translated by L. F., and "At the Florists," by Jacques Prévert, translated by L. F.

139. The Nation, Vol. 184, No. 8. New York, N.Y., The Nation Company, February 23, 1957.

Edited by M. L. Rosenthal. Contains "Rooks." Collected as #19 in *A Coney Island of the Mind*.

140. Hearse, No. 1. Eureka, Calif., 1957.

Contains "Open City," a reproduction of a painting by Lawrence Ferlinghetti.

141. Evergreen Review, Vol. I, No. 2. New York, N.Y., Grove Press, Inc., 1957.

Edited by Barney Rosset and Donald Allen. Contains "From: A Coney Island of the Mind," nos. 4, 9, and 14, and "Dog." Photo of of the poet by Harry Redl.

142. Evergreen Review, Vol. I, No. 4. New York, N.Y., Grove Press, Inc., 1957.

Edited by Barney Rosset and Donald Allen. Contains the article "Horn on '*Howl*.'" Collected in *A Casebook on the Beat*, and *Structure and Style*.

143. Coastlines #8, Vol. 2, No. 4. Hollywood, Calif., California Quarterly, Inc., Autumn, 1957.

Edited by Mel Weisburd. Contains "A Few Cool Words for 'Howl'."

144. Ark III. San Francisco, Calif., Ark, Winter, 1957.

Edited by James Harmon. Contains "Frame This Picture." Uncollected.

145. Chicago Review, Vol. 12, No. 1. Chicago, Ill., Spring, 1958.

Edited by Paul Carroll. Contains the article, "Note on Poetry in San Francisco," and the poem, "And the Arabs," which is #6 in *Pictures of the Gone World*.

146. The Nation, Vol. 186, No. 16. New York, N.Y., The Nation Company, April 19, 1958.

Edited by M. L. Rosenthal. Contains "What Happened the Day a Poet Was Appointed Postmaster." Uncollected.

147. Chicago Review, Vol. II, No. 4. Chicago, Ill., Winter, 1958.

Edited by Paul Carroll. Contains "A Picture of the Gone World."

148. Big Table, Vol. I, No. 3. Chicago, Ill., Big Table, Inc., 1959.

Edited by Paul Carroll. Contains "from HER," an excerpt from Ferlinghetti's novel, *Her*.

149. Vindrosen. n.p. [Copenhagen, Denmark], Gyldenal, Ltd., May, 1959.

Contains "Billeder fra en svunden verden" [No. 5. in *Pictures of the Gone World.*]

150. San Francisco Review 2. San Francisco, Calif., R. H. Miller, 1959.

Edited by R. H. Miller. Contains "Museum of Objects Depicting the History of My Race." Uncollected.

151. Lunes De Revolucion, Cuba, May 16, 1959.

Edited by Guillermo Cabrera Infante. Contains "En Un Año Surrealista" [No. 4 in *A Coney Island of the Mind.*]

152. Beatitude #4. San Francisco, Calif., John Kelley, May 30, 1959.

Edited by John Kelley. Contains "Loud Prayer." Uncollected.

153. Big Table, Vol. 1, No. 2. Chicago, Ill., Big Table, Inc., Summer, 1959.

Edited by Paul Carroll. Contains "The Great Chinese Dragon." Collected in *Starting from San Francisco*. The back cover consists of a photograph of Ferlinghetti.

154. Beatitude #5. San Francisco, Calif., John Kelley, June 6, 1959.

Edited by John Kelley. Contains "Venice, After the War." Uncollected.

155. The Nation, Vol. 189, No. 4, New York, N.Y., The Nation Company, August 15, 1959.

Edited by M. L. Rosenthal. Contains "An Autumn in a Word." Uncollected.

156. Beatitude #8. San Francisco, Calif., Bread and Wine Mission, August 15, 1959.

Edited by Pierre Delattre. Contains "Page of Writing from *HER*."

157. Beatitude #12. San Francisco, Calif., Bread & Wine Mission, December, 1959.

Edited by Pierre Delattre. Contains "page of writing from *HER.*"

158. L'Express. Paris, France, February 18, 1960.

Contains "Par une annee surrealiste" [No. 4 in *A Coney Island of the Mind.*]

159. Revista de la Universidad de Mexico. Mexico City, Mexico, March, 1960.

Contains "Puerto Escondida" [The Hidden Door]. Translated by Luis Oyarzún and Jose Miguel Oviedo.

160. Evergreen Review, Vol. 4, No. 12. New York, N.Y., Grove Press, Inc., March-April, 1960.

Edited by Barney Rosset. Contains "He." Collected in *Starting from San Francisco*.

161. Les Lettres Nouvelles 4. Paris, France, Julliard, June, 1960.

Edited by Maurice Nadeau. Contains "Des fois . . ." [No. 5 in *A Coney Island of the Mind.*]

24

162. Between Worlds: An International Magazine of Creativity, Vol. I, No. 1. Denver, Colorado, Inter American University by Alan Swallow, Summer, 1960.

Edited by Gilbert Neiman. Contains "Flying Away." Collected in *Starting from San Francisco*.

163. Beatitude #16. San Francisco, Calif., July 13, 1960.

Edited by Alan Dienstag. Contains "Big Fat Hairy Vision of Evil." Collected in *Starting from San Francisco*.

164. Evergreen Review, Vol. 4, No. 15. New York, N.Y., Evergreen Review, Inc., 1960.

Edited by Barney Rosset. Contains "Hidden Door." Collected in *Starting from San Francisco*.

165. Svetova Literatura 4. Prague, Czechoslovakia, 1960.

Edited by Jan Rezac. Contains thirteen poems from *A Coney Island of the Mind*, in Czechoslovakian, with illustrations, followed by a photograph of the poet.

166. Chelsea 8. New York, N.Y., Chelsea Foundation, Inc., 1960.

Edited by Ursule Molinaro, Sonia Raiziss, Venable Herndon, and Alfredo de Palchi. Contains "Political Poem." Uncollected.

167. Beatitude 17. San Francisco, Calif., City Lights Books, October-November, 1960.

Edited by Lawrence Ferlinghetti. Contains "Overpopulation," collected in *Starting from San Francisco*, several fillers, and "The Screwtop Letters," which are made up letters.

168. Swank, Vol. 7, No. 5. New York, N.Y., Royal Publications, Inc., November, 1960.

Edited by M. Jonathan Starr. Contains "I Am Waiting." Collected in *A Coney Island of the Mind*.

169. Liberation: An Independent Monthly, Vol. VI, No. 1. New York, N.Y., March, 1961.

Contains the essay, "Poet's Notes on Cuba." Uncollected.

170. Revista de la Universidad de Mexico. Mexico City, Mexico, April, 1961.

Contains "Superpoblacion" [Overpopulation]. Collected in *Starting from San Francisco*.

171. The Carolina Quarterly, Vol. 13, No. 2. Chapel Hill, No. Carolina, University of No. Carolina, Spring, 1961.

Contains "A Night Landscape." Uncollected.

172. Evergreen Review, Vol. 5, No. 18. New York, N.Y., Evergreen Review, Inc., May-June, 1961.

Edited by Barney Rosset. Contains "One Thousand Fearful Words for Fidel Castro." Published originally as a broadside. Collected in *Starting from San Francisco.*

173. Il Contemporaneo, Vol. IV, No. 37. Rome, Italy, June, 1961.

Edited by Eugenio Rizzi. Contains "Mille paro timorose per Fidel Castro." Same as preceding entry.

174. Revista de la Universidad de Mexico. Mexico City, Mexico, July, 1961.

Contains "Un Coney Island die Espiritu, No. 1," "Retratos del Mundo Ido, No. 12," and "Cristo Se Bajó" [Christ Climbed Down]. Translated by Ernesto Cardenal. All previously published.

175. Journal for the Protection of All Beings, No. 1. San Francisco, Calif., City Lights Books, 1961.

Edited by Michael McClure, Lawrence Ferlinghetti, and David Meltzer. Contains the story, "Picturesque Haiti." Uncollected.

176. The Outsider, Vol. I, No. 1. New Orleans, La., Loujon Press, Fall, 1961.

Edited by Jon Edgar Webb. Contains "Underwear." Collected in *Starting from San Francisco.*

177. Nuova Presenza 7-8. Milan, Italy, Autumn, 1962.

Edited by Magenta Varese. Contains "Egli" [He], from *Starting from San Francisco.* Translated by Roberto Sanesi.

178. Renaissance, Vol. I, No. 4. San Francisco, Calif., Renaissance Publications, 1962.

Edited by John Bryan. Contains the prose-poem, "A Parade Tirade." Collected in *New Directions in Prose and Poetry 18.*

179. Liberation: An Independent Monthly, Vol. VII, No. 10. New York, N.Y., December, 1962.

Contains "A Parade Tirade." See preceding entry.

180. Evergreen Review, Vol. 6, No. 24. Evergreen Review, Inc., May-June, 1962.

Edited by Barney Rosset. Contains " 'Lower' California," an article about Baja, by and with charcoal drawings by Ferlinghetti.

181. Konkret. Munich, Germany, June, 1962.

Contains "Berlin." Originally published as a broadside.

182. Evergreen Review, Vol. 6, No. 27. New York, N.Y., Evergreen Review, Inc., November-December, 1962.

Edited by Barney Rosset. Contains "The Man Who Rode Away." Uncollected.

183. Eco Contemporaneo, Vol. I, No. 4. Buenos Aires, Argentina, December, 1962.

Edited by Miguel Grinberg. Contains "Descripcion Experimental de una cena dada para promover el Enjuiciamiento del Presidente Eisenhower."

184. Root and Branch: A Radical Quarterly. Berkeley, Calif., Winter, 1962.

Contains the poem, "Berlin: A Note on My Poetics." Uncollected.

185. Evergreen Review, Vol. 7, No. 28. New York, N.Y., Evergreen Review, Inc., January-February, 1963.

Edited by Barney Rosset. Contains "Spurt Blood," a play by Antonin Artaud, translated by L. F.

186. Youth, Vol. 14, No. 8. St. Louis, Mo., United Church Press, April 14, 1963.

Edited by Herman C. Ahrens, Jr. Contains "Sometime During Eternity." Collected as #5 in *A Coney Island of the Mind.*

187. City Lights Journal, Number One. San Francisco, Calif., City Lights Books, 1963.

Edited by Lawrence Ferlinghetti. Contains the prose piece, "The Road to Topolobampo." Uncollected.

188. Poets at the Metro, Vol. 5. New York, N.Y., Dan Saxon, June, 1963.

Contains the titled drawing, *For the marriage and those two Corsos.*

189. Ylioppilaslehti. Helsinki, Finland, August 3, 1963.

Contains "Sielun Linnanmaelta" [No. 5 in *A Coney Island of the Mind.*] Translated by Anselm Hollo. Also a photo.

190. Information & Documents. Paris, France, September 15-October, 1963.

Contains an excerpt from *La Quatrieme Personne du Singular* [*Her*].

191. Red Clay Reader. Charlotte, No. Carolina, Southern Review, 1964.

Edited by Charleen Whisnant. Contains the drama, "The Jig Is Up." Collected in *Routines.*

192. City Lights Journal, Number Two. San Francisco, Calif., City Lights Books, 1964.

Edited by Lawrence Ferlinghetti. Contains the plays, "His Head," "Ha-Ha," and "Non-Objection." Illustrations by Roland Topor. All three plays collected in *Routines*.

193. Carolina Quarterly, Vol. XVII, No. 1. Chapel Hill, North Carolina, Fall, 1964.

Edited by Timothy Perkins and Dave Canalos. Contains "A Night Landscape." Uncollected.

194. Les Temps Modernes, No. 223. Paris, France, R. Julliard, December, 1964.

Edited by Jean Paul Sartre. Contains "Il" [He], from *Starting from San Francisco*.

195. Politica. Mexico, D.F., December 15, 1964.

Contains "Mie Palabras Pusilanimes Para Fidel Castro."

196. Fuck You /A Magazine of the Arts, Vol. 8, No. 5. Ed Sanders, March, 1965.

Edited by Ed Sanders. Contains "To Fuck Is to Love Again." Revised and collected.

197. El Rehilete, No. 13. Mexico City, Mexico, El Rehilete, April, 1965.

Contains the play, "Los Soldados de Ningun Pais" [The Soldiers of No Country], from *Unfair Arguments with Existence*.

198. Kulturní Tvorba. Císlo, Czechoslovakia, 1965.

Contains "The Man Who Rode Away." Collected in *Poetry Festival* and *Poesia Degli Ultimi Americani*.

199. Crononauta 2. Mexico City, Mexico, n.d. [1965?].

Edited by Alexandro Jodorowsky and Rene Rebetez. Contains the play, "Victimas de la Amnesia," from *Unfair Arguments with Existence*.

200. Bulletin from Nothing, Number One. San Francisco, Calif., Spring, 1965.

Edited by Claude Pelieu. Contains the prose-poem, "Telegram from Spain."

201. New Statesman, Vol. LXX, No. 1794. London, England, The Statesman & Nation Publishing Co. Ltd., July 30, 1965.

Contains the prose-poem, "Where Is Vietnam?"

28

202. Fux Magascene. San Francisco, Calif., Ari Publications, 1965.

Edited by Robert Branaman. Contains "To Fuck Is to Love Again." Revised and collected.

203. Liberation: An Independent Monthly, New York, N.Y., September, 1965.

Edited by Dave Dellinger. Contains "Where Is Vietnam?"

204. Isis, No. 20. Oxford, England, Robert Maxwell for Oxford University, October, 1965.

Edited by Andrew Lawson. Contains an untitled poem on the sculptor, Giacometti. Uncollected.

205. Tydskrif Vir Letterkunde. Johannesburg, Africa, November, 1965.

Edited by Abel Coetzee. Contains "Drie Meisies Gaan Oor Die Land" [No. 16 from Pictures of the Gone World]. Translated by Marié Blomerus.

206. Cahiers des Midis, No. 12. Namur, Belgium, November, 1965.

Edited by Jean Renson. Contains "Le Monde est Merveilleux" [No. 11 in A Coney Island of the Mind].

207. Phantomas. Brussels, Belgium, December, 1965.

Editor-in-Chief: Theodore Koenig. Contains "3 Poemes Spontanes Sur La Force De Frappe De L'Amour A Six Heures Du Matin" [3 Spontaneous Poems on the Striking Force of Love at 6 o'Clock in the Morning]. Uncollected.

208. Randstad 10. Amsterdam, Netherlands, De Bezige Bij, 1966.

Edited by Hugo Claus, Ivo Michiels, Harry Mulisch, Simon Vinkenoog. Contains nos. 6, 9, 10, 13, 24, from Pictures of the Gone World, translated by Rudi Wesselius, and "Sometime During Eternity" [No. 5 in A Coney Island of the Mind], translated by Rosey Pool and Rudi Wesselius, and "Underwear," from Starting from San Francisco, translated by Rudi Wesselius. Photo of Ferlinghetti on back cover.

209. The Transatlantic Review, No. 21. London, England, Joseph McCrindle, Summer, 1966.

Contains a drawing by the poet and "Tate Gallery, London, July 1965." Uncollected.

BOOK APPEARANCES

210. HOWL OF THE CENSOR, edited by J. W. Ehrlich. San Carlos, Calif., Nourse Publishing Company, 1956.

Gray cloth over boards in the dust jacket. Ferlinghetti was the defendant in the trial, being the publisher of Howl and Other Poems, by Allen Ginsberg.

211. NEW DIRECTIONS IN PROSE AND POETRY 16. New York, N.Y., A New Directions Book, 1957.

Red cloth over boards in the dust jacket. Contains Nos. 1, 2, and 13 from *A Coney Island of the Mind*, which was in galley form when this anthology was compiled.

212. JAM SESSION: AN ANTHOLOGY OF JAZZ, edited by Ralph J. Gleason. New York, N.Y., G. P. Putnam's Sons, 1958.

Red cloth over boards in the dust jacket. Contains an excerpt from "Autobiography," from *A Coney Island of the Mind*.

213. THIS KIND OF BIRD FLIES BACKWARD, by Diane Di Prima. New York, N.Y., Totem Press, 1958.

Decorative wrappers. Cover by Fred Herko. Drawings by Bret Rohmer. Contains "A Non-Introduction by Way of Introduction."

214. THE BEATS, edited by Seymour Krim. Greenwich, Conn., Fawcett Publications, Inc. (Gold Medal Books), March, 1960.

Pictorial wrappers. Contains No. 5 from *A Coney Island of the Mind*.

215. THE BEAT SCENE, edited by Elias Wilentz, New York, N.Y., Corinth Books, distributed by the Citadel Press, 1960.

Pictorial wrappers. Contains "Tentative Description of a Dinner Given to Promote the Impeachment of President Eisenhower." Also, five photos of the poet.

216. BEATITUDE ANTHOLOGY, edited by Lawrence Ferlinghetti. San Francisco, Calif., City Lights Books, 1960.

Pictorial wrappers. Contains "Loud Prayer," and "Page of Writing from *Her*." This is the only book appearance for "Loud Prayer."

217. THE NEW AMERICAN POETRY: 1945-1960, edited by Donald M. Allen. New York, N.Y., Grove Press, Inc., 1960.

Clothbound in dust jacket, and in decorative wrappers [two editions]. Contains Nos. 8, and 23 from *Pictures of the Gone World*, and Nos. 1, 11, and 15 from *A Coney Island of the Mind*, and "He."

218. TRENTE-CINQ JEUNES POETES AMERICAINS, edited and translated by Alain Bosquet. Paris, France, Gallimard, 1960.

Printed wrappers. Contains "Not Too Long," No. 5 from *Pictures of the Gone World*.

219. TIGER, words selected by Lyle E. Linville, photographed by James C. Hansen. Cortland, Ohio, Linville-Hansen Associates, Inc., 1961.

Pictorial wrappers, spiral bound. A first printing of 200 copies only. Contains excerpts from three of Ferlinghetti's poems.

220. THE CALIFORNIANS: Writings of Their Past and Present, Vol. II, edited by Ursule Spier Erickson and Robert Pearsall. San Francisco, Calif., Hesperian House, 1961.

Green cloth over boards in the dust jacket. Contains "Dog," and "They Were Putting Up the Statue." Both poems are from *A Coney Island of the Mind*.

221. A CASEBOOK ON THE BEAT, edited by Thomas Parkinson. New York, N.Y., Thomas Y. Crowell Company, 1961.

Black cloth over boards in the dust jacket. The dust jacket serves as the wrapper cover for the paperback edition. Contains "Overpopulation," from *Starting from San Francisco*; "Constantly Risking Absurdity," from *A Coney Island of the Mind*, and "Note on Poetry," and "Horn on *Howl*." The last two are prose pieces and are collected here in their only book appearances.

222. JUNGE AMERIKANISCHE LYRIK, edited by Gregory Corso and Walter Hollerer. Munich, Germany, Carl Hanser, 1961.

Wrappers in slipcase, with 45 r.p.m. record inserted. Contains "He," Nos. 8, 17, and 18, from *A Coney Island of the Mind*, and "Dog." This is the first book appearance for "He" which was collected in *Starting from San Francisco*. Ferlinghetti reads "Dog" on the 45 r.p.m. record.

223. 'BEAT' POETS, selected by Gene Baro. London, England, Vista Books (The Pocket Poets), 1961.

Wrappers. Contains "Away Above a Harborful," No. 1 in *Pictures of the Gone World*, and "In Paris in a Loud Dark Winter," No. 4 in *Pictures of the Gone World*, and "Constantly Risking Absurdity," No. 15 in *A Coney Island of the Mind*.

224. NEW DIRECTIONS 17 IN PROSE AND POETRY, edited by J. Laughlin. New York, N.Y., A New Directions Book, 1961.

Clothbound and pictorial wrappers [two editions]. Contains "Euphoria," "Hairy Man," and "Cro-Magnons." This is the only printing for the last two poems.

225. IDAN JA LANNEN RUNOT. Helsinki, Finland, Weilin & Goos, 1962.

Green cloth over boards in the dust jacket. Translated by Markku Lahtela and Anselm Hollo. Contains "Yks paiva iaisyydessa," and "Alati uhmaten Mielettomyytta ja kuolemaa," nos. 5 and 15 from *A Coney Island of the Mind*.

226. POETRY FESTIVAL (COMMISSIONED POEMS, 1962). San Francisco, Calif., Poetry Center, San Francisco State College, 1962.

Decorative wrappers. Poems read at the Poetry Festival held at San Francisco Museum of Art from June 21 through June 24 ,1962. Contains "The Man Who Rode Away."

227. PENGUIN MODERN POETS 5. London, England, Penguin Books, Ltd., 1963.

> Decorative wrappers. Contains "In Goya's Greatest Scenes," "Sometimes During Eternity," "Dove sta Amore," "Autobiography," "Big Fat Hairy Vision of Evil," "He," "Underwear," "Come lie with me and be my love," and "One Thousand Fearful Words for Fidel Castro." The first two poems are from *A Coney Island of the Mind*, the remaining are from *Starting from San Francisco*.

228. MEAT SCIENCE ESSAYS, by Michael McClure. San Francisco, Calif., City Lights Books, July, 1963.

> Decorative wrappers. Contains the introduction by Ferlinghetti, "A Note on MEAT SCIENCE ESSAYS."

229. NUESTRA DECADA: *La Cultura Contemporanea a Traves de Mel Textos (Revista de la Universidad de Mexico)*, Vol. I. Mexico, D.F., Universidad Nacional Autonoma de Mexico, 1964.

> Black cloth over boards. Contains "Un Coney Island del Espíritu No. 1," "Retratos del Mundo Ido #12," and "Cristo se Bajo" [Christ Climbed Down]. Translated by Ernesto Cardenal.

230. NEW DIRECTIONS IN PROSE AND POETRY 18, edited by J. Laughlin. New York, N.Y., A New Directions Book, 1964.

> Pictorial wrappers. "Thoughts of a Concerto of Telemann," "Parade Tirade," "Berlin," and the play, "Servants of the People." This is the only book printing for "Parade Tirade."

231. SAN FRANCISCO RENAISSANCEN; Elleve Moderne Amerikanske Lyrikere, edited by Redigeret af Erik Thygesen. Copenhagen, Denmark, Sirius, 1964.

> Wrappers. Contains nos. 1, 2, 3, 4, 5, 6, 7, 8, and 9, from *A Coney Island of the Mind*, "Kristus Klatrede Ned" [Christ Climbed Down], and "Hunden" [Dog].

232. POESIA DEGLI ULTIMI AMERICANI, a cura di Fernanda Pivano. Milano, Italy, Le Comete 35, Feltrinelli Editore, November, 1964.

> Pictorial wrappers. Contains "Berlin," "Big Fat Hairy Vision of Evil," and "The Man Who Rode Away."

233. GARLANDS FOR CHRISTMAS: A Selection of Poetry, edited by Chad Walsh. New York, N.Y., The Macmillan Company, 1965.

> Printed wrappers. Contains "Christ Climbed Down."

32

234. POETRY OF OUR TIME: An Introduction to Twentieth-Century Poetry, Including Modern Canadian Poetry, edited by Louis Dudek. Toronto, Canada, The Macmillan Company of Canada Limited, 1965.

Printed wrappers. Contains "Constantly risking absurdity," from A Coney Island of the Mind.

235. LA POESIE DE LA BEAT GENERATION. Paris, France, Denoel, 1965.

Printed wrappers. Translated by Jean-Jacques Lebel. Contains "Mille Mots Anxieux Pour Fidel Castro," "Les Acrobates de Picasso," "Oui," "Je Vous Présente Miss Metro," "Et les Arabes" [the second half of this poem was deleted], "Le Ciel" [Heaven], "Il" [He], and "Les Monde Est Merveilleux" [The World Is a Wonderful Place].

236. WHOLLY COMMUNION: The Film by Peter Whitehead (Poetry at the Royal Albert Hall, London, June 11th, 1965). London, England, Lorrimer Films Limited, 1965.

Pictorial wrappers. The front cover consists of a photograph of Ferlinghetti reading, which is a segment from the film that was made from the reading as described in the title. Contains "To Fuck Is to Love Again."

237. MODERN EUROPEAN POETRY, edited by Willis Barnstone. New York, N.Y., Bantam Books, Inc. (A Bantam Classic), January, 1966.

Wrappers. Contains translations by Ferlinghetti of seven poems by Jacques Prévert.

238. SOLITUDES, by Bob Kaufman. Paris, France, Union Générale D'Editions (Series 10/18), March, 1966.

White printed wrappers. Translated by M. G. Beach and Claude Pelieu. Contains "Telegram—Preface" by Ferlinghetti.

239. STRUCTURE AND STYLE: An Analytical Approach to Prose Writing, by Harriet W. Sheridan, New York, N.Y., Harcourt, Brace & World, Inc., 1966.

Printed wrappers. Contains "Horn on Howl."

240. HOPSCOTCH, by Julio Cortázar. New York, N.Y., Pantheon Books, 1966.

Clothbound in dust jacket. Page 486 contains an excerpt from A Coney Island of the Mind.

PHONOGRAPH RECORDINGS

241. SAN FRANCISCO POETS. Evergreen Records, Lp, No. EVR-1, New York, 1957. Contains booklet of poems recorded and photos of the poets. (Now distributed by Hanover Records, New York.)

Lawrence Ferlinghetti reads his poem, "Dog."

242. JAZZ CANTO: An Anthology of Poetry and Jazz, Vol. 1. World Pacific Records, Lp, No. WP-1244. Hollywood, Calif., December, 1958.

Lawrence Ferlinghetti's poem "Dog" is read by Bob Dorough, with The Bob Dorough Quintet, music by Bob Dorough.

243. POETRY READINGS AT THE CELLAR WITH THE CELLAR JAZZ QUINTET, by Kenneth Rexroth and Lawrence Ferlinghetti. February, 1958.

Fantasy 7002. 33-1/3 Lp. n.p. [San Francisco, Calif.], n.d. [February, 1958]. The drawings of the two poets on the front cover are from photographs.

244. FANTASY RECORDS HI-FI SAMPLER.

Fantasy FS-654. 33-1/3 Lp. n.p. [San Francisco, Calif.], n.d. [March, 1958]. Ferlinghetti reads his poem, "Statue of St. Francis." This track is an excerpt from the preceding entry.

245. TENTATIVE DESCRIPTION OF A DINNER TO PROMOTE THE IMPEACHMENT OF PRESIDENT EISENHOWER AND OTHER POEMS.

Fantasy 7004. 33-1/3 Lp. n.p. [San Francisco, Calif.], n.d. [August, 1958]. The photograph of the poet on the front cover is by Harry Redl. The back cover of the jacket contains an article by Ferlinghetti.

246. ALLEN GINSBERG LAWRENCE FERLINGHETTI GREGORY CORSO ANDREI VOZNESENSKY

Lovebooks LB0001. 33-1/3 Lp. London, England, 1965. Photos of the poets appear on the front cover. A short blurb on the back cover of the jacket is by Ferlinghetti. Lawrence Ferlinghetti reads two of his poems: "Bus Trip to New York-Albany," and "Underwear."

247. LAWRENCE FERLINGHETTI READING AT BETTER BOOKS.

Better Books. 33-1/3 Lp. London, England, 1965. Published in a limited edition of 100.

CRITICISM

San Francisco Chronicle, This World, Sunday, October 16, 1955.

Contains "Among the New Books," by Kenneth Rexroth, which includes a review of *Pictures of the Gone World*.

34

The New York Times Book Review. September 2, 1956.

Page 7 contains "West Coast Rhythms," by Richard Eberhart, which is the first published article on the Beats.

Evergreen Review, Vol. I, No. 2. New York, N.Y., Grove Press, Inc., 1957.

Edited by Barney Rosset and Donald Allen. Pages 5-14 contain "San Francisco Letter," by Kenneth Rexroth.

Poetry, Vol. 90, No. 4. Chicago, Ill., Poetry, July, 1957.

Edited by Henry Rago. Pages 260-261 contain a letter to Ferlinghetti from the editor, defending City Light's publication of Allen Ginsberg's, *Howl and Other Poems*.

Down Beat, Vol. 24, No. 17. Chicago, Ill., Charles Suber, August 22, 1957.

Edited by Jack Tracy. Page 34 contains "Perspectives," by Ralph J. Gleason.

Life, Vol. 43, No. 11. Chicago, Ill., Time, Inc., September 9, 1957.

Pages 105-109 contain the article, "Big Day for Bards at Bay."

Saturday Review, Vol. XL, No. 40. New York, N.Y., Saturday Review, Inc., October 5, 1957.

Pages 5-7 contain the column "Trade Winds," by John G. Fuller.

Commentary, Vol. 24, No. 6. New York, N.Y., American Jewish Committee, December, 1957.

Edited by Elliot E. Cohen. Pages 475-9 contain "America's 'Angry Young Men'; How Rebellious Are the San Francisco Rebels?," by Dan Jacobson.

The Reporter, Vol. 17, No. 10. New York, N.Y., The Reporter Magazine Company, December 12, 1957.

Edited by Max Ascoli. Contains "How Captain Hanrahan Made 'Howl' a Best Seller," by David Perlman.

Library Journal, Vol. 83, No. 12. New York, N.Y., R. R. Bowker Co., June 15, 1958.

Edited by Lee Ash. Pages 1937-1938 contain a review of *A Coney Island of the Mind*, by Gerald D. McDonald. Pages 1850-1854 contain "California's Young Writers, Angry and Otherwise," by Basil Ross.

The New York Times Book Review, Vol. LXIII, No. 36. New York, N.Y., The New York Times Company, September 7, 1958.

Page 10 contains "Five Voices in Verse," by Harvey Shapiro, which includes a review of *A Coney Island of the Mind*.

Coastlines #11, Vol. 3, No. 3. Hollywood, Calif., California Quarterly, Inc., Autumn, 1958.

Edited by Gene Frumkin. Pages 46-47 contain a review of *A Coney Island of the Mind*, by Gene Frumkin.

The Nation, Vol. 187, No. 11. New York, N.Y., The Nation Company, October 11, 1958.

Edited by Robert Hatch. Pages 214-5 contain "The Naked and the Clad," by M. L. Rosenthal, which includes a review of *A Coney Island of the Mind*.

Playboy, Vol. 5, No. 11. Chicago, Ill., HMH Publishing Co., November, 1958.

Pages 30-32 contain a parody of "A Coney Island of the Mind," by John D. Keefauver.

Poetry, Vol. 93, No. 2. Chicago, Ill., Poetry, November, 1958.

Edited by Henry Rago. Contains "Four New Books," by Hayden Carruth, which includes a review of *A Coney Island of the Mind*.

THE HOLY BARBARIANS, by Lawrence Lipton. New York, N.Y., Julian Messner, Inc., 1959.

Clothbound in dust jacket. Chapter 12 contains material on Ferlinghetti. Photo.

Pegasen. Uppsala, Sweden, 1959.

Edited by Lars Kleberg. Pages 20-22 contain "San Francisco Beat Generation." The first paragraph is in English, the remainder in Swedish.

Liberation: An Independent Monthly, Vol. IV, No. 4. New York, N.Y., June, 1959.

Contains: "After the Beat Generation: Hipsters Unleashed," by David McReynolds.

The Observer, London, England, Sunday, November 1, 1959.

Contains "Bearding the Beats," by Kenneth Tynan. Photo.

The Spectator, No. 6856. London, England, November 20, 1959.

Pages 720-721 contain "A Poet for Christmas," by D. J. Enright, which includes a review of *A Coney Island of the Mind*.

Library Journal, Vol. 85, No. 3. New York, N.Y., R. R. Bowker Co., November 15, 1960.

Edited by Eric Moon. Page 363 contains "The Emphasis Is on a Single Character," an article about Ferlinghetti.

New Statesman, Vol. LVIII, No. 1500. London, England, The Statesman & Nation Publishing Co. Ltd., December 12, 1959.

Page 850 contains a review of *A Coney Island of the Mind*, by G. S. Fraser.

L' Express. Paris, France, February 18, 1960.

Page 32 contains the article "La Bombe Atomique et Les Poètes," by Alain Bosquet.

The Study of English 3. Tokyo, Japan, The Kenkyusha Publishing Co., March, 1960.

Pages 44-48 contain "San Francisco Beat Generation," in Japanese. Photo.

New York Post. April 14, 1960.

Contains "Beatnik Poem Stirs Row at Oyster Bay College," by Jack O'Grady. The poem in question was No. 5 from *A Coney Island of the Mind*.

New York Journal-American. April 14, 1960.

Contains "Calls Beatnik Poem Ridicule of Christ," by Scott Morton.

New York World Telegram. April 14, 1960.

Contains "Probe Reading in State College of Beatnik Poem on Crucifixion," by Robin Turkel.

New York Times. April 14, 1960.

Contains "Poem Read in Class Stirs Inquiry Here."

Newsday. Thursday, April 14, 1960.

Contains "Call 'Beat' Poem at College Blasphemy," by Si Radiloff.

The New York Times. Friday, April 15, 1960.

Contains "L. I. Inquiry Begun on Disputed Poem."

New York World Telegram and Sun. April 15, 1960.

Contains "Sick Sacrilege."

Long Island Daily Press. April 15, 1960.

Contains "Poems Defended by Profs, Critics; Attacked by CWV."

Newsday. April 15, 1960.

Contains "Beatnik Poet Protests Charge of Blasphemy," by Si Radiloff. Photo.

The New York Times. April 16, 1960.

Contains "Poem Episode Decried."

New York Times. April 17, 1960.

Contains "L. I. Dean Is Hailed for Stand on Poem."

The Commonweal. New York, N.Y., The Commonweal Publishing Co., Inc., April 29, 1960.

Page 118 contains "On Reading Modern Poetry."

New York Civil Liberties Union, Vol. VIII, No. 5. June, 1960.

Page 1 contains "NYCLU Defends Right to Read Beatnik Poetry."

Svetova Literatura 4. Prague, Czechoslovakia, 1960.

Edited by Jan Rezác. Contains an article in Czechoslovakian by Jan Rezác.

Library Journal, Vol. 85, No. 20. New York, N.Y., R. R. Bowker Co., November 15, 1960.

Edited by Eric Moon. Page 4162 contains a review of *Her*, by Dorothy Nyren.

The Washington Post, Sunday, October 23, 1960.

Page 3 contains "The Beats (Who Really Never Were) Are Gone," by James McC. Truitt. Photo.

Beatitude 17. San Francisco, Calif., City Lights Books, Oct.-Nov., 1960.

Edited by Lawrence Ferlinghetti. Contains the letter to Ferlinghetti, "Part of a Letter from LeRoi Jones," dated September 28, 1960.

The Commonweal, Vol. LXXIII, No. 19. New York, N.Y., The Commonweal Publishing Co., Inc., February 3, 1961.

Pages 488-489 contain "A Novel from the World of Modern Beatdom," a review of *Her*, by Martin Tucker.

Syndicats. Brussels, Belgium, February 12, 1961.

Contains a review of *La Quatrième Personne du Singulier* [*Her*], by Jacques Cabau.

Les Beaux Arts. Brussels, Belgium, March 2, 1961.

Contains a review of *La Quatrième Personne du Singulier* [*Her*].

San Francisco Sunday Chronicle, This World, March 5, 1961.

Page 27 contains "Ferlinghetti's 'Her'—Just Give In to It Like a Lady," a review of *Her*, by Vincent McHugh. Photo.

The Minnesota Review, Vol. I, No. 4. Minneapolis, Minn., The Minnesota Review, July, 1961.

Pages 504-505 contain a review of *Her*, by Daniel Leary.

The Christian Century: An Undenominational Review, Vol. LXXVIII, No. 28. Christian Century Foundation, July 12, 1961.

Edited by Harold E. Fey. Page 854 contains "Toward Rebirth," a review of *Her*, by Stanley J. Rowland, Jr.

38

The San Francisco Examiner, Highlights, Sunday, September 24, 1961.

Page 2 contains "Soft Covering a Revolution." Photo.

Figaro Littéraire. Paris, France, November 11, 1961.

Contains a review of *La Quatrième Personne du Singular* [*Her*], by Robert Kanters.

Paris Normandie. Paris, France, December, 1961.

Contains a review of *La Quatrième Personne du Singular* [*Her*], by Pierre La Page.

L' Express. Paris, France, December, 1961.

Contains a review of *La Quatrième Personne du Singular* [*Her*], by Jacques Cabau. Photo.

Kansas City Star. Saturday, January 6, 1962.

Contains "A Fresh Voice in Poetry, to Be Read and Heard," a review of *Starting from San Francisco*, by Webster Schott.

Oakland Tribune, Sunday, January 28, 1962.

Contains "Ferlinghetti Writes at His Impish Best," a review of *Starting from San Francisco*, by Jack Anderson.

The Fresno Bee, Fresno, Calif., February 4, 1962.

Contains "Poems That Will Curl Your Hair," a review of *Starting from San Francisco*, by Ivan Olson.

The Village Voice, New York, N.Y., March 15, 1962.

Page 5 contains a review of *Starting from San Francisco*, by Aaron Kramer.

Ulster County Townsman, Woodstock, Ulster Co., New York, March 15, 1962.

Contains "Olive Post Censures Use of Poem at OCS." The poem in question is No. 5 in *A Coney Island of the Mind*. Also contained is "Teacher Clarifies," a letter to the editor from Fernando J. Valdivia, a high school teacher, defending the poem.

San Francisco Examiner, Sunday, March 18, 1962.

Contains "A Poetic Shorthand to Be Read Aloud," a review of *Starting from San Francisco*, by Mark Linenthal.

The Kingston Daily Freeman, Kingston, New York, March 20, 1962.

Contains "Speakers Give Views on Controversial Poem."

Ulster County Townsman, Woodstock, Ulster County, New York, Thursday, March 22, 1962.

Pages 1, 3-4, 8 contain "Board Backs Principal After Spirited Session," by Marian Umhey.

The Crusader, Friday, March 23, 1962.

Page 3 contains an interview with Ferlinghetti by Lu Mezzeta.

San Francisco Chronicle, This World, Sunday, March 25, 1962.

Page 30 contains "The Pulsing Voices of the New Poets," by James Schevill, which includes a review of *Starting from San Francisco*.

Library Journal, Vol. 87, No. 7. New York, N.Y., R. R. Bowker Co., April 1, 1962.

Edited by Eric Moon. Page 1470 contains a review of *Starting from San Francisco*, by Dorothy Nyren.

The New York Times Book Review, Vol. LXVII, No. 17. New York, N.Y., The New York Times Company, April 29, 1962.

Page 30 contains "Fresh Patterns of Near Rhymes," by X. J. Kennedy, which includes a review of *Starting from San Francisco*.

Saturday Review, Vol. XLV, No. 18. New York, N.Y., Saturday Review, Inc., May 5, 1962.

Pages 24-27 contain "Experience in Image, Sound, and Rhythm," by James Schevill, which includes a review of *Starting from San Francisco*.

Poetry, Vol. 100, No. 5. Chicago, Ill., Poetry, August, 1962.

Edited by Henry Rago. Pages 314-316 contain reviews of *Starting from San Francisco* and *Berlin*, by Alan Dugan.

The New York Times Book Review, September 9, 1962.

Contains "Between Verses: Report on a West Coast Poetry Festival," by Jack Gilbert.

The New York Times Book Review, September 16, 1962.

Contains "Vanishing Beat," by Raymond Walters, Jr.

Konkret. Munich, Germany, March, 1963.

Page 24 contains a letter to the editor concerning Ferlinghetti's *A Coney Island of the Mind*.

New York Times Western Edition, Tuesday, March 12, 1963.

Contains "N. Y. Groups Seen in 3 New Dances; Sophie Maslow's 'Poem' Is an Instant Hit," by Allen Hughes. The choreography is from passages of Ferlinghetti's poem, "Autobiography."

Voices: A Journal of Poetry, No. 180. Vinalhaven, Maine, January-April, 1963.

Page 54 contains a review of *Starting from San Francisco* by John Fandel.

Yale Daily News, New Haven, Conn., Thursday, May 9, 1963.

Contains "Ferlinghetti: Purple Poet or Boring Beat?" Two articles: "Coney Island Hotdogs Taste Real Phony," by John H. Garabedian, and " 'Cheese, Please Cookies,' Says Poet in Interview," by S. M. L. Aronson.

Deutsche Zeitung, May 25-26, 1963.

Contains a review of *Sie* [*Her*], by Hans-Jurgen Heise.

The Observer Weekend Review, London, England, June 2, 1963.

Contains "Beat in London," by Paul Ferris. Photo.

Rheinische Post, July 10, 1963.

Contains a review of *Sie* [*Her*], by Alexander Baldus.

Tagerspiegel, Sunday, July 21, 1963.

Contains a review of *Sie* [*Her*], by Wolfgang Maier.

Ylioppilaslehti. Helsinki, Finland, August 3, 1963.

Contains an article on Ferlinghetti and a photograph.

Information & Documents. Paris, France, September 15-October, 1963.

Pages 10-11 contain an interview with Ferlinghetti in French. Photo.

Kie Literarische Tat. Zurich, Switzerland, Friday, October 18, 1963.

Contains an article by Dorothea Schlegee.

Frontier, Vol. 15, No. 2. Los Angeles, Calif., Frontier, December, 1963.

Edited by Phil Kerby. Pages 18-20 contain the article "The Political Role of the Artist," by Lawrence Lipton, which is devoted almost entirely to the reviewing of *Meat Science Essays*, by Michael McClure. The introduction that Ferlinghetti wrote for this book is discussed.

The Times Literary Supplement, Thursday, January 2, 1964.

Contains a review of *Penguin Modern Poets*.

S.F. Examiner, The California Weekly, People, Sunday, February 2, 1964.

Page 4 contains *Snapshots:* "Lawrence Ferlinghetti," by Horace Schwartz, an anecdotal article with caricature sketch.

San Francisco Chronicle, February 16, 1964.

Contains "A Beat-up World Hanging by Its Fingernails," a review of *Unfair Arguments with Existence*, by Vincent McHugh. Photo.

New York Times, Tuesday, April 26, 1964.

Contains "Dancing, Poetry and Jazz Are Fused in 'Poem'," by Allen Hughes, about Sophie Maslow's performed choreography of Ferlinghetti's poem, "Autobiography."

Drama Critique, Spring, 1964.

Edited by Hugh Dickinson. Contains a review of *Unfair Arguments with Existence*, by Patrick Henry.

New Mexico Quarterly, Vol. XXXIV, No. 1. Albuquerque, New Mexico, The University of New Mexico Press, Spring, 1964.

Edited by Richard C. Angell. Page 117 contains a review of *Unfair Arguments with Existence*, by Richard C. Angell.

Chinese World, San Francisco, Calif., Thursday, May 14, 1964.

Contains the editorial, "Ferlinghetti Strikes It Rich."

Poetry, Vol. 104, No. 4. Chicago, Ill., Poetry, July, 1964.

Edited by Henry Rago. Contains "Seven Poets and a Playwright," by Dabney Stuart, which includes a review of *Unfair Arguments with Existence*.

Nation, Vol. 199, No. 8. New York, N.Y., The Nation Company, September 28, 1964.

Edited by Carey McWilliams. Contains "Letter from Prague," by Robert Littel.

San Francisco Chronicle, December 9, 1964.

Contains "The Tragedy at the Greek Theatre," by Ralph J. Gleason, an article about the free speech movement on the Berkeley campus, in which dialogue from Ferlinghetti's play, "Servants of the People," is quoted.

Encilla, Santiago, Chile, April, 1965.

Page 32 contains "Beatniks y Jóvenes Iracundos," by Ariel Dorfman. Photo.

The Carleton Miscellany, Vol. VI, No. 2. Northfield, Minn., Carleton College, Spring, 1965.

Edited by Erling Larsen. Page 112 contains a review of *Routines*.

El Nacional Papel Literano, Caracas, South America, April 11, 1965.

Contains "El Ultimo Libro de Laurence Ferlinghetti," a review of *Routines*.

Palo Alto Times, Palo Alto, Calif., Saturday, April 24, 1965.

Contains "Ferlinghetti drama set at Foothill in benefit program for rights cause." An article about the play, "The Soldiers of No Country." Photos of players.

Vinduet Redigeret af Beat Grasten. n.p. [Finland?], May, 1965.

Contains "Madonnaer af Kod og af Aud," an article about Ferlinghetti by Erik Thygesen. Two photos.

The New York Times, Monday, June 7, 1965.

Contains "Ogden Nash's Verses Charm Russians," by Theodore Shabad. Ferlinghetti is mentioned and six lines from his poem, "Dog," are quoted.

La Tour De Feu. Jarnae, France, 1965.

Edited by Pierre Boujut. Contains the article, "Poésie et Publicité," by Serge Fauchereau.

San Francisco Chronicle, Monday, June 14, 1965.

Page 6 contains "Strange Sounds and Profanity, London Meets the Beats," about reading at Royal Albert Hall in London. Photo.

New Statesman, London, England, June 18, 1965.

Page 950 contains "London 'Diary' ," by Francis Hope, about reading at Royal Albert Hall in London.

The Sunday Times, London, England, June 20, 1965.

Page 41 contains "A Voice at Large," by Edward Lucie-Smith, and article-interview with Ferlinghetti.

The London Magazine, August, 1965.

Contains "Poetry, Sold Out," by Hugo Williams, an article about reading at Royal Albert Hall in London.

The Sunday Herald Tribune, Book Week, Vol. 2, No. 48. New York, N.Y., Herald Tribune, Inc., August 8, 1965.

Page 15 contains a review of *Routines* by Gilbert Sorrentino.

Penthouse: The Magazine for Men, Vol. I, No. 4. London, England, Penthouse Publications, Ltd., August, 1965.

Edited by Bob Guccione. Pages 24, 26, 71-3 contain the interview by Thaddeus Vane, "Lawrence Ferlinghetti: A Candid Conversation with the Man Who Founded the Beat Generation." Photo.

The Sunday Herald Tribune, Book Week, Vol. 2, No. 48. New York, N.Y., Herald Tribune, Inc., August 8, 1965.

Page 15 contains a review of *Routines* by Gilbert Sorrentino.

San Francisco Chronicle, Friday, August 13, 1965.

Contains "Conference at S.F. State: Hayakawa's Semantical Rescue." Also photo of Ferlinghetti and comments about and quotes from his reading of his poem, "Where Is Vietnam?"

Saturday Review, Vol. XLVIII, No. 36. New York, N.Y., Saturday Review, Inc., September 4, 1965.

Contains "The San Francisco Beat," by Haskel Frankel.

The Idiot, No. 4. San Francisco, Calif., Michael-john Publications, December, 1965.

Edited by James Wojack. Pages 9, 10-11, 14-20 contain "The Idiot Interview with Lawrence Ferlinghetti."

Poetry, Vol. 108, No. 2. Chicago, Ill., Poetry, May, 1966.

Edited by Henry Rago. Pages 125-6 contain a review of *Routines* by Richard Duerden.

GARY SNYDER

Gary Snyder

 GARY SNYDER WAS BORN May 8, 1930, at Stanford General Hospital in San Francisco. He was the first of the two children born to Harold and Lois Snyder. The family remained in San Francisco for one and one-half years after their son was born and then moved to Washington.

"We moved to the Pacific Northwest in the depression and were extremely poor for quite awhile. We opened up a dairy farm with two or three dairy cows, sixty to eighty Rhode Island Reds, geese, fruit trees, and so forth—selling milk to neighbors. We were doing a little farming and my father eventually got a full-time job with the Federal Bureau of Employment working during the days and running the farm on weekends, mornings, and evenings. That was a rural area, lots of woods, and working on the farm, my sister and I had chores to do all the time. I learned to read very early, and I read a great deal, although it was my mother who actually introduced me to literature by reading poetry to me every night before I went to bed."

During this period he became interested in woodcraft, learning the names of trees and herbs, building different kinds of shelters, and learning about American Indian lore.

"I never felt deprived or annoyed by poverty, which I regarded as a minor obstruction; for it seemed we were always going to the public library to get books, and we always had dozens of books around the house. At that time we were quite a bit poorer than most of our neighbors. So what I developed was a certain amount of self-discipline and an enjoyment in doing a certain amount of work, and then a great attachment to nature."

In 1942 he moved with his family to Portland, Oregon, where he graduated from the eighth grade.

"The adjustment was a little difficult but I continued with the same interests. At that time I was intensely concerned with American Indians. I was sewing my own moccasins and spending as much time as possible out in the woods around the Columbia River, or south of Portland, camping and hiking. I took up archery at that time, too. I made my own arrows for awhile—I really thought you should be able to make your own bows and arrows and things, although I didn't get around to making my own bow. The biggest probable childhood influence on me was Ernest Thompson Seton and his

47

book of Indian woodcrafts, which have a curious mystique of the Indian and of nature, as well as a lot of funny Mickey Mouse information about how to do things."

The summers of 1943-1945 he worked in a camp at Spirit Lake, Washington.

"It was here that I got my first taste of high country and where I learned the rudiments of mountain climbing and back packing, and changed over from lowland wilderness to alpine wilderness. What I learned there I extended later into Forest Service and logging and mountaineering experience."

That fall he entered high school in Portland, and while he was writing poetry all along, "I don't remember any of that poetry very clearly except that it was all concerned with nature or youth." The summers of 1946-1947 were spent working for a radio station music library helping them program canned music. He also did considerable free-lance radio acting during that period and worked at various times for both United Press and the Portland *Oregonian* as a copy boy. It was also during this period that he was doing extensive mountain climbing as a member of the Mazamas Mountain Climbers, which was an adult club that required the climbing of a snow peak for membership, which he did at the age of fifteen.

He graduated from Lincoln High School in Portland in 1947 and that fall enrolled in Reed College. "The next summer [1948] I shipped out from New York as a seaman: I was galley man or pantry man, I forget which.

"Going to sea was part of a long growth and extension of my sympathies and sensibilities outside simply one area and to many classes and kinds of people and many parts of the world so that now I feel at home everywhere."

In 1951 he graduated from Reed College with an interdepartmental degree in Anthropology/Literature. [He was at this time married to Alison Gass, a marriage that lasted from 1950 to 1952.]

"My bachelor's thesis was concerned with both areas. I was particularly interested in mythology, folklore, and oral literature. It's curious how in my thesis I mapped out practically all my major interests and I've followed through on them ever since. Most of the things concerning my poetry are handled in there in one way or another as well as my particular approach to history, psychological problems, nature of the mind, nature of mythology, function and forms of literature, and so forth. All of these were foreshadowed there.

"Poetry was growing on me very slowly. I think probably

48

somewhere midway through my college career it became hardly fixed in my mind, and then finally after one semester at Indiana University I made a complete and total choice, consciously turning my back on the professional scholar's career in anthropology—which is where I was headed—and setting myself loose in the world to sink or swim as a poet."

The summer of 1950 was spent working for the Park Service excavating the archaeological site of old Fort Vancouver, and the summer of 1951 as a timber scaler on the Warm Springs Indian Reservation in Oregon. *Berry Feast*, the lead poem in Snyder's next book, will be dedicated to the students he lived with that summer.

He returned to San Francisco in the spring of 1952. "I worked at various jobs: I worked for Kodak and at installing burglary alarms; and then in the summer of 1952 I hitchhiked back north and worked as a lookout on Crater Mountain in the Baker National Forest." When I got back to San Francisco, Philip Whalen was in town (we'd roomed together at Reed) and we got an apartment over on Montgomery — Montgomery and Green Streets—and we shared that apartment all through 1952, until the spring of 1953. There weren't too many people to see then, just Whalen and myself, and a few old friends from Reed from time to time. Lew [Welch] was in Chicago. I didn't know too many people then. It was very quiet. I met the painter Dick Brewer, and he arranged to introduce Philip and me to Robert Duncan, and we even got on the streetcar one evening, I remember, and went to Duncan's place, but inexplicably, Duncan wasn't there and so we never met Duncan, as it turned out, until many years later. It would have been interesting to have met him at that time for he was still early in his career then, and certainly more advanced as a poet than I was at that time. There was no real poetic voice then in San Francisco. There was Rexroth, but it wasn't until the fall of 1953 that I met Rexroth for the first time.

The summer of 1953 he returned to the Mt. Baker Forest as a lookout on Sourdough Mountain. "That fall I moved to Berkeley. I was living in a little cottage and studying Chinese and Japanese at the university and going up to the woods and mountains in the summer, writing and reading. Intellectually, and in every way, that was a period of great excitement and growth for me—but a solitary period, too. I had very few friends and almost no social contacts for three or four years there. I was doing nothing but studying and working."

He started the season of 1954 as a lookout with the Packwood district of the Gifford Pinchot forest in Washington, but he was immediately fired, on orders from Washington, D.C., as a security risk. That was the end of Snyder's Forest Service career. After the logging strike of that summer was settled he went to work as a choker-setter at Camp A of the Warm Springs Lumber Company, and stayed at the camp until winter weather shut it down. The following summer he worked on a trail crew at Yosemite National Park. Part of *Riprap* came from this experience.

"I had decided in the fall of 1953 to go to Japan to study Zen Buddhism and that's what caused me to go back to graduate school in Oriental Languages in Berkeley — to prepare for that. So it was just a matter of time until I got over there.

"It was in the fall of 1955 that I met Ginsberg, and it was also in the fall of 1955 that Kerouac first came to town. Then Whalen came down from some mountain job, and Ginsberg had the idea of having a poetry reading somewhere. We hadn't had a poetry reading in years in San Francisco, it seemed. Somehow a poetry reading was held at the old Six Gallery in the Marina in October or November of 1955 and at that reading Ginsberg read *Howl* for the first time it had ever been heard in public, and I read some things, and Philip read some things, and it sort of started things going: McClure and Lamantia also read that evening, and Rexroth was the master of ceremonies. Up to that time Ferlinghetti had only published *Pictures of the Gone World*, his own book, and the next book City Lights published was *Howl*, which immediately got into the newspapers. So that was where a big blast of public consciousness of poetry came into being. But of course Duncan and Spicer had been here all the time, writing — and, of course, Rexroth."

Then in May, 1956, Snyder went to Japan for the first time on a scholarship from the First Zen Institute of America. He remained in Japan for one and one-half years, studying the language and living in a Zen temple.

"In 1957—August—I got on the *Sappa Creek* in Yokohama. I had intended to go across the Pacific, but as it turned out I worked about eight months as a wiper in the engine room. We went to the Persian Gulf five times, once to Italy, once to Turkey, once to Okinawa, once to Wake, once to Guam, once to Ceylon, and once to Pago Pago, Samoa, and Kwajalein. All those places. We were going all over the world, back and forth, sailing along at fourteen knots.

50

"That was a very interesting period. I got paid off the ship in April, 1958, in San Pedro. Then I came up to San Francisco and spent nine months here participating again in the poetry scene: meeting old friends, meeting Joanne Kyger, doing some writing, and then in the spring of 1959 I went back to Japan. A year later Joanne followed and we got married immediately afterward. Then I stayed in Japan from 1959-1965 with the exception of six months in India." His entire stay in Japan was spent in Kyoto, where he studied for five years under Oda Sesso Roshi, the Zen master and the Head Abbot of Daitoku-Ji.

"As much as the books I've read the jobs I've had have been significant in shaping me. My sense of body and language and the knowledge that intelligence and insight, sensitivity, awareness, and brilliance are not limited to educated people, or anything like it. That's why I dedicated *Riprap* to that list of fellow-workers. Those were all men I'd known as seamen on the *Sappa Creek*, that tanker; or men I'd worked with in the woods. I felt I owed them as individuals, as persons, as much as I owed any books. They were real teachers, they were all men of no education, but men of great natural brilliance and life. Some real fuck-ups too, of course. The "T-2 Tanker Blues" in *Riprap* is about that ship, and the "Sappa Creek" poem is also about that experience.

The year of 1964-1965 Gary Snyder taught in the English Department at the University of California at Berkeley. He participated in the Berkeley poetry conference of July, 1965, as a lecturer and reader. He returned to Japan to continue his study of Zen Buddhism in October of 1965.

"A poet faces two directions: one is to the world of people and language and society, and the other is the nonhuman, nonverbal world, which is nature as nature is itself; and the world of human nature — the inner world — as it is itself, before language, before custom, before culture. There's no words in that realm. There aren't any rules that we know and that's the area that Buddhism studies. You can't talk about it because it's not concerned with anything that you can talk about. The practice of it is in sitting cross-legged and meditating. That's all I can say, *Zazen*—sitting still and looking in. Whether you feel like it or not sometimes. It's not the same as poetry, but it touches in a mysterious way.

51

A poet exists in terms of others. At least in terms of one other person, if nothing else. There are two ways to relate to others and society. One is to tell society what you think is wrong, what you think is right; and the other is to *do* what you think is right, and both of these ways help. If somebody really feels a sense of being and belonging and understanding for, say some part of this continent, his very identity in being there is worth more than twenty-five people that *don't* feel it but go around talking about it."

In a statement for the Paterson Society in 1961, Snyder wrote: "As poet I hold the most archaic values on earth. They go back to the late Paleolithic: the fertility of the soil, the magic of animals, the power-vision in solitude, the terrifying initiation and re-birth, the love and ecstasy of the dance, the common work of the tribe. I try to hold both history and wilderness in mind, that my poems may approach the true measure of things and stand against the unbalance and ignorance of our times."

gary snyder
R I P R A P

a cobble of stone laid on steep slick rock
to make a trail for horses in the mountains

ORIGIN PRESS 1959

TITLE PAGE, NO. 2A, FRONT COVER, NO. 4

BOOKS, BROADSIDES, POSTERS, TRANSLATIONS

1. THE DIMENSIONS OF A MYTH. Portland, Oregon, Reed College Library, June, 1951.

   Unpublished bachelor's thesis. 3 copies only, distributed to Reed College Library, Reed College Archives, and the author.

2a. RIPRAP. Ashland, Mass., Origin Press, 1959.

   Blue and white wrappers, with white title label on front cover lettered in black. Printed and bound in Japan. 500 copies only.

2b. Reissued in 1960 in an edition of 1000 copies in brown and white wrappers, and with a title label similar to the first edition except that the title was lettered irregularly. The copyright page contains the designation *second edition.*

   ERRATA: *below* for *belown*, page [6]. *Crazy Horse Mason* has been added to the dedication, having been erroneously omitted from the first edition. The typographical error on p. [6] was also corrected for the second edition.

3a. MYTHS AND TEXTS. New York, N.Y., Totem Press, September, 1960.

   White printed wrappers, with the first letters of the title decoratively printed. All lettering in black. Cover design and drawings by Will Petersen. 1100 copies only.

3b. Reissued August, 1961, in an edition of 1100 copies. The second printing may be identified by the following points:
   1. Wrappers are slick white, with all lettering identical with the first edition except in red.
   2. The publisher's name and address were dropped from the copyright page.

   ERRATA: The epigraph on the copyright page has not been acknowledged. Two lines were omitted from the text: Page 23 should conclude with *spiderwebs in the eyes,* Page 24 should begin with *Gray chunk rocks roll down, flexible* for *inflexible,* page 42, line 6; *too* for *to,* page 43, line 4.

3c. Reissued June, 1965, in an edition of 1500 copies. All errors have been corrected for this printing, which is otherwise identical with the first edition except that, like the second printing, the publisher's name and address were dropped from the copyright page.

4. THE WODDEN FISH; Basic Sutras & Gathas of Rinzai Zen. Prepared with Kanetsuki Gutetsu. n.p. [Kyoto, Japan], The First Zen Institute of America in Japan, 1961.

Brown wrappers, with decorative title label on front cover in red. Issued with an errata slip. About 300 copies, of which only 25 copies were released for distribution in this country.

5. THE FIRING. New York, N.Y., R. L. Ross, April, 1964.

Broadside. Stone lithograph by R. L. Ross. 7 copies only. The edition was numbered and signed by the artist/publisher. Not for sale.

6. NANAO KNOWS. n.p. [San Francisco, Calif.], [Four Seasons Foundation], n.d. [June, 1964].

Broadside. Published and placed on sale as a souvenir item for the Freeway reading given by Philip Whalen, Gary Snyder, and Lew Welch. 300 copies only.

7. ACROSS LAMARCK COL. n.p. [San Francisco, Calif.], East Wind Printers (A Poetry Folio, 1964), 1964.

Broadside. Illustrated by Francesca Greene. 300 copies. Created for the San Francisco Art Festival, 1964. A series of 10 broadsides by as many poets, with each broadside having a different illustrator. The colophon for the set is on a separate sheet, and with the 10 broadsides is laid loose in a golden-brown wrapper with a fuchsia title label.

8a. HOP, SKIP, AND JUMP. n.p. [Berkeley, Calif.], Oyez, 1964.

Broadside. 350 copies only. Printed by the Auerhahn Press for Oyez. No. 9 in the publisher's series of 10 broadsides.

8b. 27 copies of each broadside in the series were later signed by the ten poets and laid in a heavy linen board folder for separate sale. Only 25 of these sets, which were prepared in 1965, were offered for sale.

9. DEAR MR. PRESIDENT. n.p. [San Francisco, Calif.], [C. Plymell and Ari Publications], n.d. [1965].

Poster. 500 copies. Printed in the poet's holograph. A petition poem for President Johnson protesting the war in Vietnam. Not for sale.

10. RIPRAP & COLD MOUNTAIN POEMS. San Francisco, Calif., Four Seasons Foundation, July, 1965.

Dark brown printed wrappers. 2000 copies printed, of which 1000 copies have been bound for the first issue. Both titles were reproduced from the original printings by offset; the Cold Mountain Poems, which are Snyder translations of poems by Han-Shan, being first published in Evergreen Review magazine. This book is Writing 7 in the publisher's series.

11. SIX SECTIONS FROM MOUNTAINS AND RIVERS WITHOUT END. San Francisco, Calif., Four Seasons Foundation, July, 1965.

Mustard yellow printed wrappers. 2000 copies printed, of which 1000 copies have been bound for the first issue. This book is Writing 9 in the publisher's series.

56

12a.   A RANGE OF POEMS. London, England, Fulcrum Press, March, 1966.

> Brown cloth over boards in the dust jacket. This is a collected edition of the poet's work, and contains: *Riprap, Cold Mountain Poems, Myths & Texts, Poems of Miyazawa Kenji*, and *The Back Country*. Half-tone drawings on three pages by Will Petersen. Cover drawing and book section drawings by Gary Snyder. Frontispiece photo of the poet by Ken Walden. 1000 copies printed, of which 500 have been bound for the first issue. Issued with an errata slip.

12b.   Special edition on Glastonbury antique laid paper numbered 1 to 100 of which the first 50 have been numbered and signed by the author. The special edition was issued with a white dust jacket in place of the brown dust jacket used for the ordinary edition.

EPHEMERA

13.   POETRY CENTER/ At San Francisco State College/ Sunday, November 23, 1958 — 8:30 p.m./ Telegraph Hill Neighborhood Assn./ presents/ PHILIP LEVINE and/ GARY SNYDER

> 8vo. mimeographed sheet. [1] p. Contains "Notes from the poets."

14.   THE EAST WEST REVIEW/ Vol. I, No. 1, Spring, 1964 [Koyoto, Japan, Doshisha University]

> Wrappers. Extract from *The East-West Review*.

15.   September 29, 1964/ THE POETRY CENTER/ San Francisco State College/ presents:/ GARY SNYDER

> 8vo. mimeographed sheet. [1] p. Contains a biographical notice and "A Statement by the Poet."

PERIODICAL CONTRIBUTIONS

> [*All contributions are poems, or translations of poems, unless otherwise noted.*]

16.   Janus, First Number. n.p. [Portland, Oregon], Reed College Student Publication, January, 1950.

> Contains "a poem." Uncollected.

17.   Janus, Vol. I, No. 2. n.p. [Portland, Oregon], Reed College Student Publication, February, 1950.

> Contains "Song." Uncollected.

18. Janus. n.p. [Portland, Oregon], Reed College Student Publication, 1950.

Contains "Autumn Equinox." Uncollected.

19. Janus, Vol. II, No. 3. n.p. [Portland, Oregon], Reed College Student Publication, February, 1951.

Contains "Sinecure for P. Whalen." Uncollected.

20. Gurgle. n.p. [Portland, Oregon], Reed College Student Publication, June, 1951.

Contains "For George Leigh Mallory / Missing on Mt. Everest," and "By the North Gate, Wind Blows Full of Sand." Both uncollected.

21. Folio, Vol. XVII, No. 2. Bloomington, Indiana, Department of English, Indiana University, March, 1952.

Contains "Song for a Four Crowned Dancing Hat." Collected in *Myths & Texts*.

22. Berkeley Bussei. Berkeley, Calif., Berkeley Young Buddhist Association, 1954.

Contains "Maitreya." Collected in *Myths & Texts*.

23. Poems and Pictures. San Francisco, Calif., Porpoise Bookshop, 1954.

Edited by Henry Evans. Contains "Hunting /12 from Myths & Texts." Collected.

24. Berkeley Bussei. Berkeley, Calif., Berkeley Young Buddhist Association, 1955.

Contains "Epistemological Fancies." Uncollected.

25. Poems and Pictures, Number Four. San Francisco, Calif., Porpoise Bookshop, July, 1955.

Edited by Henry Evans. Contains "Olympic Mountains." Collected in *Myths & Texts*.

26. Midwest Folklore, Vol. V, No. 3. Bloomington, Ind., Indiana University, 1955.

Contains the book review by Snyder of *Indian Legends of the Pacific Northwest*, by Ella E. Clark.

27. Occident. Berkeley, Calif., The University of California, Fall, 1955.

Contains "Song to Be Sung Later." Uncollected.

28. Berkeley Bussei. Berkeley, Calif., Berkeley Young Buddhist Association, 1956.

Edited by Sei Shohara. Contains "Piute Creek." Collected in *Riprap* and *Contemporary American Poetry*.

29. The Needle, Vol. I, No. 2. San Francisco, Calif., July, 1956.

Contains "Groves, 14, from Myths & Texts." Collected in *Myths & Texts*.

30. Ark II/ Moby I. n.p. [San Francisco, Calif.], James Harmon, 1956-1957.

Edited by Michael McClure and James Harmon. Contains "Groves, 12." Collected in *Myths & Texts*.

31. Evergreen Review, Vol. I, No. 2. New York, N.Y., Grove Press, Inc., 1957.

Edited by Barney Rosset and Donald Allen. Contains "The Berry Feast," collected in *The Back Country** and "North Beach Alba." Both poems were collected in *Helgon & Hetsporrar*.

32. Evergreen Review, Vol. I, No. 3. New York, N.Y., Grove Press, Inc., 1957.

Edited by Barney Rosset and Donald Allen. Contains "Letter from Kyoto." A letter describing the people and city of Kyoto. Collected in *The Beats*.

33. Berkeley Bussei. Berkeley, Calif., Berkeley Young Buddhist Association, 1957.

Edited by Mildred Okano. Contains "Late October Camping in the Sawtooths." Uncollected.

34. The Black Mountain Review 7. Black Mountain, North Carolina, Autumn, 1957.

Edited by Robert Creeley. Contains "Changes: 3." Collected in *Myths & Texts*.

35. Combustion, No. 4. Toronto, Canada, Contact Press, October-December, 1957.

Contains "Tokyo," uncollected, and "For a Far-Out Friend," collected in *Riprap* and *Contemporary American Poetry*.

36. Ark III. San Francisco, Calif., James Harmon, Winter, 1957.

Edited by James Harmon. Contains "What I Think About When I Meditate." An excerpted version appears in *The Holy Barbarians*.

37. Berkeley Bussei. Berkeley, Calif., Berkeley Young Buddhist Association, 1958.

Contains "Song for a Stone Girl at Sanchi," collected in *The Back Country*, and "For Zeami and Kwanami from Myths & Texts," collected in *Myths & Texts*.

The Back Country was to have been the title of Gary Snyder's next volume of poetry; however, these poems became a section, under the same title, in *A Range of Poems*.

59

38. Yugen, No. 2. New York, N.Y., LeRoi Jones and Hettie Cohen, 1958.

Edited by LeRoi Jones and Hettie Cohen. Contains "Chion-in." Uncollected.

39. The Fifties, No. 1. Madison, Minn., The Fifties Press, 1958.

Contains "First Shaman Song," collected in *Myths & Texts*, and "Milton by Firelight," collected in *Riprap and Contemporary American Poetry*.

40. Combustion, No. 7. Toronto, Canada, Contact Press, August, 1958.

Contains "Night," collected in *The Back Country*, "After the Chinese," uncollected, and "Cartagena," collected in *Riprap*.

41. Yugen, No. 3. New York, N.Y., LeRoi Jones and Hettie Cohen, 1958.

Edited by LeRoi Jones and Hettie Cohen. Contains "Another for the same" and "Praise for Sick Women." The last poem was collected in *Riprap* and *The New American Poetry: 1945-1960*.

42. Chicago Review, Vol. XII, No. 2. Chicago, Ill., Chicago Review, The University of Chicago Press, Summer, 1958.

Edited by Irving Rosenthal. Contains "Spring Sesshin at Shokoku-ji," and essay describing life in a Zen temple during a special week of meditation. Collected in *The World of Zen*.

43. Evergreen Review, Vol. II, No. 6. New York, N.Y., Grove Press, Inc., Autumn, 1958.

Edited by Barney Rosset and Donald Allen. Contains "Cold Mountain Poems," which are Snyder translations of "Twenty-four Poems by Han-Shan," and the "Preface to the Poems of Han-Shan by Lu Ch'iu, Governor of T'ai Prefecture." Included are Snyder's introduction and notes. Collected in *Riprap* and *Cold Mountain Poems*.

44. Jabberwock. Edinburgh, Scotland, Edinburgh University Review, 1959.

Edited by Alex Neish. Contains "From Myths & Texts: burning/ 15; hunting/ 16." Collected in *Myths & Texts*.

45. Liberation: An independent monthly, Vol. IV, No. 4. New York, N.Y., June, 1959.

Contains the essay, "Note on the Religious Tendencies." Collected in *The Beats*.

46. Yugen, No. 4. New York, N.Y., LeRoi Jones and Hettie Cohen, 1959.

Edited by LeRoi Jones. Contains "From Myths & Texts." Collected in *Myths & Texts*.

47. San Francisco Review, Vol. I, No. 2. San Francisco, Calif., San Francisco Review, Spring, 1959.

Edited by R. H. Miller. Contains "The Late Snow & Lumberstrike of the Summer of Fifty-Four." Collected in *Riprap, A Casebook on the Beat*, and *Poets of Today*.

48. Evergreen Review, Vol. III, No. 9. New York, N.Y., Grove Press, Summer, 1959.

Edited by Barney Rosset. Contains "Night," collected in *The Back Country*, and "Cartagena," collected in *Riprap*.

49. Foot, No. 1. San Francisco, Calif., Foot, n.d. [September, 1959].

Edited by Richard Duerden. About 300 copies only. Contains two letters from Gary Snyder to Richard Duerden. Uncollected.

50. Vigil: A New Writing by New Writers, Vol. I, No. 2. Chicago, Ill., Roosevelt University, Autumn, 1959.

Edited by Arnold L. Kaye. Contains "Seven Quick Flips." Uncollected.

51. The Galley Sail Review, Vol. II, No. 1/ Issue Number 5. San Francisco, Calif., Galley Sail Publications, Winter, 1959-1960.

Edited by Stanely McNail and Guest Editor, David Rafael Wang. Contains "Hunting," and "This Poem Is for Deer," both collected in *Myths & Texts*, and "Kyoto Sketch," uncollected.

52. Big Table, Vol. I, No. 4. Chicago, Ill., Big Table, Inc., Spring, 1960.

Edited by Paul Carroll. Contains "The Manichaeans." Collected in *The Back Country*.

53. San Francisco Review, Vol. I, No. 4. San Francisco, Calif., R. H. Miller, 1960.

Edited by R. H. Miller. Contains "Vapor Trails." Collected in *The Back Country* and 'Beat' Poets.

54. Poems from the Floating World, Vol. II. New York, N.Y., Hawk's Well Press, 1960.

Edited by Jerome Rothenberg. Contains "A Green Limb." Collected in *Myths & Texts*.

55. Between Worlds, Vol. I, No. 1. Denver, Colorado, Inter-American University, Summer, 1960.

Contains "A Dry Day Just Before the Rainy Season," "The Rainy Season," and "Vapor Trails." The last poem was collected in *The Back Country* and 'Beat' Poets.

56. Yugen, No. 6. New York, N.Y., LeRoi Jones and Hettie Cohen, 1960.

Edited by LeRoi Jones. Contains "A Walk," "Wild Horses," and "On Vulture Peak." "A Walk" was collected in *The Back Country*.

57. Nomad. Culver City, Calif., Nomad, Autumn, 1960.

Edited by Donald Factor and Anthony Linick. Contains "Burning the Small Dead." Uncollected.

58. Poetry Score. Carmel, Calif., Poetry Score, Fall, 1960.

Edited by Jehanne Carlson. Contains "Sixth Month Song in the Foothills," "The Lookouts," "Baker's Cabin 1952," "The Feathered Robe," "This Poem is for Birds, from 'Myths & Texts,' " "Numerous Broken Eggs," and "Under the Skin of it." All uncollected but "This Poem is for Birds."

59. Journal of American Folklore, Vol. 74, No. 291. Montpelier, Vermont, The Capital City Press, January-March, 1961.

Edited by Dell H. Hymes. Pages 82-83 contain the book review by Snyder of *Li Sao, A Poem on Relieving Sorrows*, by Ch'u Yuan, translated by Jerah Johnson.

60. Outburst 2. San Francisco, Calif., Origin, July, 1961.

Edited by Cid Corman. Contains "Bubbs Creek Haircut," "Pine River," "Yase: September," and letters to Allen Ginsberg, Will Petersen, and Philip Whalen. These letters include statements about architecture, politics, literature, "Mountains and Rivers Without End," and impressions of Istanbul and Japan. "Bubbs Creek Haircut" was collected in *Six Sections from Mountains and Rivers Without End*. "Pine River" and "Yase: September" were collected in *The Back Country*.

61. Trobar 2. Brooklyn, New York, George Economou, 1961.

Edited by George Economou, Joan Kelley, and Robert Kelley. Contains "Fire in the Hole." Collected in *The Back Country*.

62. Kulchur 3. New York, N.Y., Kulchur Press, Inc., 1961.

Edited by Marc Schleifer. Contains the essay, "The Ship in Yokohama," being a selection from a letter to Jack Kerouac.

63. The Outsider, Vol. I, No. 1. New Orleans, La., Loujon Press, Fall, 1961.

Edited by Jon Edgar Webb. Contains "Xrist." Collected in *The Back Country*.

64. Journal for the Protection of All Beings, No. 1. San Francisco, Calif., City Lights Books, 1961.

Edited by Michael McClure, Lawrence Ferlinghetti, and David Meltzer. Contains the essay, "Buddhist Anarchism." Uncollected.

65. Origin, No. 4. San Francisco, Calif., Origin, January, 1962.

Contains "Night Highway Ninety-Nine." Collected in *Six Sections from Mountains and Rivers Without End.*

66. Foot Magazine, No. 2. Berkeley, Calif., Foot Magazine, 1962.

Edited by Richard Duerden and William Brown. Contains "More Better." Uncollected.

67. The Floating Bear #22. New York, N.Y., The Floating Bear, 1962.

Edited by Diane di Prima. Contains "The Curse." Uncollected.

68. Nation, Vol. CXCV, No. 17, New York, N.Y., The Nation Company, November 24, 1962.

Edited by David Ignatow. Contains "Mother of the Buddhas, Queen of Heaven, Mother of the Sun; Marici, Goddess of the Dawn." Collected in *The Back Country.*

69. Liberation: An Independent Monthly, Vol. VII, No. 10. New York, N.Y., December, 1962.

Contains "Oil." Collected in *Seeds of Liberation* and *The Back Country.*

70. City Lights Journal, No. 1. San Francisco, Calif., City Lights Books, 1963.

Edited by Lawrence Ferlinghetti. Contains "A Journey to Rishikesh & Hardwar." This excerpt from a journal and a letter of 1962 describes Snyder's travels in India with his wife, Allen Ginsberg, and Peter Orlovsky. Uncollected.

71. The Yale Literary Magazine, Vol. CXXXI, Nos. 3 and 4. New Haven, Conn., Yale Literary Society, April, 1963.

Edited by Michael G. Gill. Contains "Four at Sea," and "The Levels." The last poem was collected in *The Back Country.*

72. Nation, Vol. 196, No. 6. New York, N.Y., The Nation Company, February 9, 1963.

Edited by David Ignatow. Contains "Asleep on the Train." Uncollected.

73. Evergreen Review, Vol. VII, No. 29. New York, N.Y., Evergreen Review, Inc., April, 1963.

Edited by Barney Rosset. Contains "The Public Bath." Collected in *The Back Country.*

63

74. The Outsider, Vol. I, No. 3. New Orleans, La., Loujon Press, Spring, 1963.

Edited by Jon Edgar Webb. Contains "Some Square Comes," and "Madly Whirling Downhill." Both uncollected.

75. Northwest Review, Vol. VI, No. 3. Eugene, Oregon, University of Oregon Student Publications Board, Summer, 1963.

Edited by Edward van Aelstyn. Contains "Eight Sandbars on the Takano River," and "Foxtail Pine." Both poems were collected in *The Back Country* and *A Controversy of Poets.*

76. The Beloit Poetry Journal, Vol. XIV, No. 1. Beloit, Wis., The Beloit Poetry Journal, Fall, 1963.

Contains "A Heifer Clambers Up." Collected in *The Back Country.*

77. Fuck You/A Magazine of the Arts, Vol. 4, No. 5. New York, N.Y., Ed Sanders, 1963.

Edited by Ed Sanders. Contains "Hymn to the Goddess San Francisco in Paradise." Collected in *Six Sections from Mountains and Rivers Without End.* This poem later appeared in the *City Lights Journal,* No. 2, 1964.

78. Origin 12. Kyoto, Japan, Origin, January, 1964.

Edited by Cid Corman. Contains "The Market." Collected in *Six Sections from Mountains and Rivers Without End.*

79. Orient West, Vol. IX, No. 1. Tokyo, Japan, January-February, 1964.

Contains "Spring and the Ashura," by Miyazawa Kenji, translated by Snyder. Uncollected.

80. Cleft, Vol. I, No. 2. London, England, May, 1964.

Contains "The Old Dutch Woman." Collected in *The Back Country.*

81. Joglars, Vol. I, No. 1. Providence, R.I., Joglars, Spring, 1964.

Edited by Clark Coolidge and George Palmer. Contains "Love has many facets." Uncollected.

82. Coyote's Journal #1. Eugene, Oregon, Coyote's Journal, 1964.

Edited by James Koller and Edward van Aelstyn. Contains "The Spring," and "April." "The Spring" was collected in *The Back Country.*

83. The East-West Review, Vol. I, No. 1. Koyoto, Japan, Doshisha University, Spring, 1964.

Edited by Naozo Ueno. Contains "3 Poems by Miyazawa Kenji," translated by Gary Snyder.

84. Evergreen Review, Vol. VIII, No. 34. New York, N.Y.,
Evergreen Review, December, 1964.

Contains "Maya," collected in *The Back Country*.

85. Synapse 3. Berkeley, Calif., Synapse, January, 1965.

Edited by D. R. Hazelton. Contains "August Was Foggy," and "Sather." Both poems were collected in *The Back Country*.

86. The Yale Literary Magazine, Vol. CXXXIII, No. 5. New
Haven, Conn., Yale Literary Society, April, 1965.

Editor-in-Chief: Edward Muller. Contains "The Plum Blossom Poem," and "Beneath My Hand and Eye the Distant Hills, Your Body." Both poems were collected in *The Back Country*.

87. Synapse 4. San Francisco Issue. Berkeley, Calif., Synapse, May, 1965.

Edited by D. R. Hazelton. Contains "For the West." Collected in *The Back Country*.

88. The Paris Review, No. 34. Paris, France, The Paris Review, Spring-Summer, 1965.

Edited by Thomas Clark. Contains "Hop, Skip, & Jump," "On Our Way to Khajuraho," and "August Was Foggy." All three poems were collected in *The Back Country*.

89. The Arizona Quarterly, Vol. 21, No. 2. Tucson, Arizona,
The University of Arizona, Summer, 1965.

Edited by Albert Frank Gegenheimer. Contains the book review by Snyder of *Where Four Worlds Meet: Hindu Kush, 1959*, by Fosco Maraini.

90. Fux Magascene. San Francisco, Calif., Ari Publications,
1965.

Edited by Robert R. Branaman. Contains "Nanao Knows." Collected in *The Back Country*.

91. Harper's Magazine, Vol. 230, No. 1381. New York, N.Y.,
Harper & Row, June, 1965.

Editor-in-Chief: Jolen Fischer. Contains "Ami Pete 24:XII:62." Collected in *The Back Country*.

92. Vietnam Blues. San Francisco, Calif., Bindweed Press,
n.d. [1965].

Edited by Robert Peterson. Contains "Dear Mr. President." Origin-ally published as a poster.

93. Poetry, Vol. 106, Nos. 1-2. Chicago, Ill., Poetry, 1965.

Edited by Henry Rago. Contains "Through the Smoke Hole." Collected in *The Back Country*.

94. Wild Dog #17. San Francisco, Calif., Wild Dog, June 8, 1965.

Edited by Drew Wagnon, Gino Clays, and Joanne Kyger. Contains "Journeys." Collected in *Six Sections from Mountains and Rivers Without End*.

95. Coyote's Journal #4. Eugene, Oregon, Coyote's Journal, 1965.

Edited by James Koller, Edward van Aelstyn, and William Wroth. Contains "To the Chinese Comrades." Uncollected.

96. Niagara Frontier Review. Buffalo, N.Y., Frontier Press, Inc., Spring-Summer, 1965.

Edited by Harvey Brown. Contains "How to Make Stew in the Pinacate Desert / Recipe for Locke and Drum." Collected in *The Back Country*.

97. Poetry Northwest, Vol. VI, No. 4. Seattle, Wash., University of Washington, Winter, 1965-1966.

Edited by Carolyn Kizer. Contains "January," "Nansen," and "Mt. Hiei." All uncollected.

98. Wild Dog, Vol. III, No. 21. San Francisco, Calif., Wild Dog, March 1, 1966.

Edited by Drew and Terry Wagnon. Contains "Hitch Haiku." Uncollected.

BOOK APPEARANCES

99. JAPAN: THEME AND VARIATIONS; A Collection of Poems by Americans. Rutland, Vermont and Tokyo, Japan, Charles E. Tuttle Co., 1959.

Contains "A Stone Garden," from *Riprap*.

100. THE HOLY BARBARIANS, by Lawrence Lipton. New York, N.Y., Julian Messner, Inc., 1959.

Clothbound in dust jacket. Contains an excerpted version of "What I Think About When I Meditate."

101. THE WORLD OF ZEN: An East-West Anthology, by Nancy Wilson Ross. New York, N.Y., Random House, 1960.

Contains the article, "Spring Sesshin at Shokoku-ji."

66

102. HELGON & HETSPORRAR; Poesi fran Beat Generation och San Franciscorenassansen, edited by Reidar Ekner. Stockholm, Sweden, Rabén & Sjogren, 1960.

Decorative wrappers. Contains "North Beach: Alba," and "Berry Feast." The last poem was collected in *The Back Country*.

103. THE NEW AMERICAN POETRY: 1945-1960, edited by Donald M. Allen. New York, N.Y., Grove Press, Inc., 1960.

Clothbound in dust jacket, and in decorative wrappers [two editions]. Contains "Praise for Sick Women," "Riprap," "For a Far-Out Friend," and "This Tokyo," from *Riprap*, and "Part III: Burning," from *Myths & Texts*.

104. THE BEATS, edited by Seymour Krim. Greenwich, Conn., Fawcett Publications, 1960.

Wrappers. Contains "Letter from Kyoto," and "Note on the Religious Tendencies."

105. A CASEBOOK ON THE BEAT, edited by Thomas Parkinson. New York, N.Y., Thomas Y. Crowell Company, 1961.

Decorative wrappers. Contains "The Late Snow and Lumber Strike of the Summer of Fifty-Four," from *Riprap*, and "Spring Sesshin at Shokoku-ji," and "Harshan."

106. JUNGE AMERIKANISCHE LYRIK, edited by Gregory Corso and Walter Hollerer. Munich, Germany, Carl Hanser, 1961.

Wrappers in slipcase, with 45 rpm record inserted. Contains in bilingual text: "Makings."

107. 'BEAT' POETS, selected by Gene Baro. London, England, Vista Books / The Pocket Poets, Longacre Press Limited, 1961.

Wrappers. Contains "Vapor Trails," collected in *The Back Country*, and "Nooksack Valley," from *Riprap*.

108. CONTEMPORARY AMERICAN POETRY, edited by Donald Hall. Baltimore, Maryland, Penguin Books, 1962.

Wrappers. Contains "All Through the Rains," "Piute Creek," "Above Pate Valley," "Milton by Firelight," and "Hay for Horses." All of the poems are from *Riprap*.

109. TIGER, words selected by Lyle E. Linville, photographed by James C. Hansen. Cortland, Ohio. Linville-Hansen Associates, Inc., 1961.

Pictorial wrappers, spiral bound. Contains an excerpt from "Praise for Sick Women," from *Riprap*.

110. BIITO SHISHU, edited and translated by Yuzuru Katagiri. Tokyo, Japan, 1963.

[This item has not been inspected by the compiler and it is not known which poems by Snyder it contains.]

111. POETS OF TODAY: A New American Anthology, edited by Walter Lowenfels. New York, N.Y., International Publications, 1964.

Clothbound in dust jacket and in decorative wrappers, the paperback title being the subtitle of the clothbound edition. Contains "The Late Snow and Lumber Strike of the Summer of Fifty-Four," from *Riprap*.

112. POESIA DEGLI ULTIMI AMERICANI, a cura di Fernanda Pivano. Milano, Italy, Le Comete 35, Feltrinelli Editore, November, 1964.

Pictorial wrappers. Bilingual text on facing pages. Contains "Toji," "Higashi Hongwanji," from *Riprap*, and "The Burning." The last poem is from *Myths & Texts*.

113. 12 POETS & 1 PAINTER, edited by Donald M. Allen. San Francisco, Calif., Four Seasons Foundation, 1964.

Decorative wrappers. This is *Writing 3* in the publisher's series. Contains "7:VII." Collected in *The Back Country*.

114. SEEDS OF LIBERATION, edited by Paul Goodman. New York, N.Y., George Braziller, 1964.

Contains "Oil." Green cloth over boards in the dust jacket. Collected in *The Back Country*.

115. A CONTROVERSY OF POETS; an Anthology of Contemporary American Poetry, edited by Paris Leary and Robert Kelley. Garden City, N.Y., Doubleday & Co., Anchor Books, 1965.

Wrappers. Contains "Hunting," "The Market—from Mts. & Rivers," and "Foxtail Pine," and "Eight Sandbars on the Takano River," collected in *The Back Country*.

CRITICISM

Liberation: An Independent Monthly, Vol. IV, No. 4. New York, N.Y., June, 1959.

Contains "After the Beat Generation: Hipsters Unleashed," by David McReynolds.

Beat Zen, Square Zen, and Zen, by Alan W. Watts. San Francisco, Calif., City Lights Books, 1959.

Pages 16-17 are concerned with Gary Snyder.

Poetry, Vol. XCVI. Chicago, Ill., Poetry, 1960.

Edited by Henry Rago. Pages 244-246 contain the review by Robert S. Sward, "Poetry Chronicle."

Prairie Schooner, Vol. XXXIV, No. 4. Winter, 1960-1961.

Pages 383-386 contain a review of *Myths & Texts* by Thomas Parkinson.

Poetry, Vol. XCVII. Chicago, Ill., Poetry, February, 1961.

Edited by Henry Rago. Pages 316-320 contain the review of *Myths & Texts* by James Dickey entitled "Five Twist Books."

Journal of American Folklore, Vol. 74, No. 292. Montpelier, Vermont, The Capital City Press, April-June, 1961.

Edited by Dell H. Hymes. Page 184 contains a review of *Myths & Texts* by Dell H. Hymes.

Sixties, No. 6. Madison, Minn., The Sixties Press, Spring, 1962.

Edited by Robert Bly. Pages 25-42 contain the critical article by Crunk, "The Work of Gary Snyder." Crunk is a pseudonym.

Américas, Vol. XVI. Washington, D.C., January, 1964.

Pages 28-32 contain the review by Lee Holland, "Homer and the Dragon: U. S. Poetry Before and After the Beats."

San Francisco Chronicle, Thursday, June 11, 1964.

Page 29 contains *Monique's Daily Mail:* "He's Living a Life of Zen and Poetry." An interview with Gary Snyder by Monique Benoit.

The Suspect in Poetry, by James Dickey. Madison, Minn., The Sixties Press, 1964.

Pages 102-103 contain the subchapter, Gary Snyder.

San Francisco Sunday Chronicle, October 11, 1964.

Page 37 contains the article on Snyder, "A Poet's Values," by Helen Breger.

Harper's Magazine, Vol. 230, No. 1381. New York, N.Y., Harper & Row, June, 1965.

Pages 65-71 contain the article by Kenneth Rexroth "The New American Poets." Gary Snyder is given prominent mention.

Epoch: A Magazine of Contemporary Literature, Vol. XV, No. 1. Ithaca, New York, Cornell University, Fall, 1965.

Pages 88-96 contain the critical article, "The Poetry of Gary Snyder," by Richard Howard.

A Biographical Sketch and Descriptive Checklist of Gary Snyder, by David Kherdian. Berkeley, Calif., Oyez, November, 1965.

Green printed wrappers. Frontispiece photo by Don Allen. Issued with an erratum sheet. 500 copies only. Designed and printed by Graham Mackintosh.

Holiday, Vol. 39, No. 3. Philadelphia, Pa., The Curtis Publishing Company, March, 1966.

Edited by Don A. Schanche. Pages 147-151 contain the article by Kenneth Rexroth, "A Hope for Poetry." Gary Snyder is given prominent mention.

PHILIP WHALEN

Philip Whalen

123 BEAVER STREET is the downstairs apartment of an old oblong Victorian house in the Mission District of San Francisco. Philip Whalen has been living here since 1963. House-guests and quarter-sharers have come and gone; e.g., Richard Brautigan, Allen Ginsberg, and Lew Welch. The downstairs apartment is divided into two one-room apartments and one two-room apartment; the kitchen and bathroom being shared. Rumor has it that Philip Whalen began his sojourn in the front room and gradually worked his way to the room in back, where he now lives, as it is the closest room to the kitchen. Food, it would seem, is his sustenance, his security, his pastime, his faith in the future.

His many friends are fond of feeding him, for "although he is appreciative of good food he can enjoy anything set before him." The center of his universe seems to be his expanding stomach, and he regards its growing girth as a victory he has earned. His blue workmen's shirts concede and defer to its size by exposing the man between buttons.

What little money comes his way seems to be spent in only two other ways: books and toys; and, like Joe in *The Time of Your Life*, he believes he can do no further harm to the already sorry state of man's affairs on earth if only he refuses to leave his chair.

Poised and self-assured he sits like Joe, in The Chair of His Life, in scorn of the world out there—flapping his arms at the doors and windows, beyond which lies the "reality" he is forever railing against. His friends, who he insists are a source of irritation and displeasure to him

> The minute I'm out of town
> My friends get sick, go back on the sauce
> Engage in unhappy love affairs

are, in truth, the great protectors of his inner world, not only by accepting him without equivocation, but by acting as buffers against the reality-world he chooses to avoid. They bring him the food of love (and often sustenance) and he, his paternal instincts long mellowed to avuncular good cheer and subtle and fanciful wit, returns their thoughfulness with his own gentle understanding.

73

Many poets today look on themselves as the saviors and martyrs of their time. Whalen, on the contrary, is not concerned with revolutions and social panaceas. If he sees the big man at all he sees him in the small situation: tripping over a pebble on his journey to deliver a rose. Out of themes that are often seemingly mundane and prosaic he creates poetry of significance because his vision is peculiarily his own and because the clarity of his intelligence is capable of grasping and arresting meaning in seemingly ephemeral and unimportant subjects. He has an ear for conversational language that reveals those absurd convictions which render him immune to any belief in sweeping changes. For Whalen, social responsibility means friendship in a field of limited reaction. The power of action is nonexistent. There is no decision or choice, only "discovery," as he puts it. The "I" that speaks is the occasional "I" behind the particular impression; hence, his world is directionless, without beginning or end. The questions he poses himself do not arise from moral considerations. Its

Not I love or hate:

but

WHAT IS IT I'M SEEING?
&
WHO'S LOOKING?

This "seeing" involves an assimilation of trivia that mounts from poem to poem. Conversation picked up at parties serves a purpose, centered as it is around a personal mystique that has to do with the clichés and dogma of his youth and a Pantheon which includes Victorian aunts and uncles. His act of propitiation before these ancestral divinities consists of perfecting their inane speech patterns in a slightly altered context. The voices, usually anonymous, recall the echoes of that earlier period. When not actually speaking himself his persona becomes diluted. He *is* the conversation that passes around him. One suddenly feels there is no choice to be made, no real situation to alter. It's always been like this. The poet cannot indicate the possibility of change when there is nothing to compare by. Hence, his time-feeling is unalterable. This petty talk, heard as if on a phonograph record, is the world. There are no moral crises, no wars, etc., only this vague eternal sing-song. The poet, adamant in his passivity, becomes his situation. His watery journey precludes no shore. This is his immortality.

74

PHILIP WHALEN

Self-Portrait,
From Another
Direction

1959
AUERHAHN PRESS

LIKE I SAY
POEMS

Philip Whalen

TOTEM PRESS
in association with
CORINTH BOOKS
32 West Eighth Street
New York 11, New York

TITLE PAGES, NOS. 3 AND 5A

BOOKS, BROADSIDES, POSTERS

1. THREE SATIRES. n.p. [Portland, Oregon], [Philip Whalen], May, 1951.

    Hand-stitched sand-colored printed wrappers. [8] pp. Hand-set and printed with blockprint decorations by the author at the Reed College Graphic Arts Studio. 13 copies only, privately printed and distributed by the author.

2. THE CALENDAR: A BOOK OF POEMS. Portland, Oregon, Reed College Library, June, 1951.

    Unpublished bachelor's thesis. 3 copies only, distributed to Reed College Library, Reed College archives, and the author.

3. SELF-PORTRAIT FROM ANOTHER DIRECTION. San Francisco, Calif., Auerhahn Press, October, 1959.

    Folded folio broadside mounted in terra-cotta printed wrappers. Hand-set and printed by Jay McIlroy and Dave Haselwood. About 1000 copies only.

4a. MEMOIRS OF AN INTERGLACIAL AGE. San Francisco, Calif., The Auerhahn Press, March, 1960.

    Stiff gray wrappers, with cover wood-block cuts by Robert LaVigne in green. Hand-set and designed by Dave Haselwood and Jay McIlroy. 1200 copies only, of which

4b. 100 copies were hardbound in text weight paper which is heavier but otherwise identical with the wrapper covers, and with a black cloth spine that is gilt lettered. Of these specially bound 100 copies

4c. 25 contained original drawings and a short poem on the flyleaf by the author, and

4d. 15 copies were signed and dated by the author on the flyleaf.

5a. LIKE I SAY. New York, N.Y., Totem Press/ Corinth Books, June, 1960.

    Gray wrappers, with cover drawing of the author in blue by Robert LaVigne running to both sides. 1000 copies.

5b. Reissued in June, 1961, in an edition of 1100 copies. The second printing may be identified by the following points:
1. Wrappers are slick white, with the drawing in red.
2. The designation, Second Printing 1961, appears on the copyright page.

6. HYMNUS AD PATREM SINENSIS. n.p. [San Francisco, Calif.], [The Four Seasons Foundation], n.d. [1963].

Broadside. A series of eight broadsides by as many poets in conjunction with the San Francisco Arts Festival. Issued in portfolio with a title label for the set on the front cover. 300 copies, of which 250 were placed for sale. Printed by George Lithograph Company.

7. THREE MORNINGS. n.p. [San Francisco, Calif.], [Four Seasons Foundation], n.d. [June, 1964].

Broadside. Published and placed on sale as a souvenir item for the Freeway reading given by Philip Whalen, Gary Snyder, and Lew Welch. 300 copies only.

8. MONDAY, IN THE EVENING, 21:VIII:61. Milano, Italy, East 128 Milano [July 20, 1964].

Red printed wrappers. Number 3 in the series, *Autori scelti da Fernando Pivano*. Front cover and text printed from silk screen reproductions of the author's holograph. Photographs of the author by Ettore Sottsass, Jr. 309 copies only, of which 291 have been numbered and placed for sale. Publication date was erroneously given as 1963, the proposed date of publication.

9a. GODDESS. San Francisco, Calif., Don Carpenter, December, 1964.

Broadside. 100 copies printed by the Auerhahn Press for the publisher as a Christmas give-away item. The opening initial was designed by the author.

9b. Also 25 copies without the colophon or opening initial for the author's personal use. These copies were lettered individually in colored ink by the poet and were to be sold by him.

10. DEAR MR PRESIDENT. n.p. [San Francisco, Calif.], [Impressions Productions], n.d. [1965].

Poster. 500 copies. Printed in the author's holograph. A petition poem for President Johnson protesting the war in Vietnam. Not for sale.

11. EVERY DAY. Eugene, Oregon, Coyote's Journal (Coyote Book #1), May, 1965.

Yellow printed wrappers. Front cover and title page were printed in the author's holograph. 600 copies only, of which 500 copies were placed for sale and 100 copies were given to the author in payment.

12. HIGHGRADE: Doodles, poems. n.p. [San Francisco, Calif.], Coyote's Journal, February, 1966.

Tan printed wrappers, with decorations in red on both sides by the author. Title page drawing by the author. Entire text in author's holograph. 460 copies only.

78

FUGITIVE PIECES AND EPHEMERA

13. SONG. n.p. n.d. [Portland, Oregon, 1951].

    Broadsheet. 2 copies only, printed by the author on a Washington Hand Press at the Graphic Arts Studio, Reed College. Both copies were printed as proof sheets on notebook paper. One copy is in the author's collection and the other has been inscribed and presented to Suzanne and Richard Duerden. Collected in *The Calendar: A Book of Poems.*

14. THE AUERHAHN PRESS [catalog]. San Francisco, Calif., The Auerhahn Press, n.d. [1959].

    Folded broadside tipped into tan printed wrappers, 7-13/16 scant x 5-2/8 inches. Contains "31:V:59." Collected in *Highgrade.*

15. Now Now Now. n.p. n.d. [San Francisco, Calif., February, 1965].

    Illustrated advertising poster, 22 x 17 inches. Composed by Charles Plymell. Contains "Lecture Notes GSS Berkeley." Collected in *Highgrade.*

16. GENTLE THURSDAY. San Francisco, Calif. [Impressions Productions], March, 1965.

    Broadsheet, 8½ x 11 inches. A mailing flyer, reproduced in the author's holograph, urging everyone to remain in their homes Thursday, March 25, 1965, to announce their desire for..."peace & quiet & liberty for all."

17. THE POETRY CENTER/ presents/ PHILIP WHALEN (October, 1965)

    8vo. mimeographed sheet. Contains *A Statement by the Poet:* by Whalen, which is reprinted from *Memoirs of an Interglacial Age.* This is the only separate printing of this statement.

PERIODICAL AND NEWSPAPER CONTRIBUTIONS

[*All contributions are poems unless otherwise noted.*]

18. Prologue. n.p. [Portland, Oregon], A Reed Student Publication, Winter, 1947.

    Edited by Frank Paul Bowman. Contains "IV," "VIII," and "XVIII." Uncollected.

19. Prologue. n.p. [Portland, Oregon], A Reed Student Publication, Spring, 1948.

    Contains *Three Desert Poems:* "The Great American Desert," "Saguaro," and "New Canaan." Uncollected.

20. Prologue. n.p. [Portland, Oregon, Reed College], February, 1949.

    Contains "From the Temptation of St. Anthony." Uncollected.

21. Prologue. n.p. [Portland, Oregon, Reed College], Summer, 1949.

Contains *The Plaster Muse: 6 Poems in the Classic Mode:* "I. Moshe Sur L'Eau," "II. Ode," "III. Leda," "IV. Thursday in Byzantium," "V. A L'Ombre Des Jeunes Filles . . ." and "VI. Sonnet for Valentine's Day." Uncollected.

22. Janus, first number. n.p. [Portland, Oregon, Reed College], January, 1950.

Contains "November First." Uncollected.

23. Janus, second number. n.p. [Portland, Oregon, Reed College], February, 1950.

Contains "An Elegy Upon the Untimely Death of Mrs. W. F.," and "Advent." Uncollected.

24. Reed College Quest. Portland, Oregon, Student Body of Reed College, Monday, February 20, 1950.

Edited by Helen Johnson. Contains the article "Volley of Verses." Uncollected.

25. Gurgle. n.p. [Portland, Oregon, Reed College], June, 1951.

Contains "Song," and "An Elegy Upon the Untimely Death of Mrs. W. F." [Revised.] Both uncollected.

26. The Poetry Book Magazine, Vol. 4, No. 1. Brooklyn, New York, Fall, 1951.

Edited by Marcia N. Holden. Contains "Meta." Collected in *The Calendar: A Book of Poems.*

27. The Poetry Book Magazine, Vol. 4, No. 4. Brooklyn, New York, Summer, 1952.

Contains "Song" and "The Road-Runner." The last poem was collected in *Like I Say.*

28. The Poetry Book Magazine, Vol. 5, No. 2. Brooklyn, New York, Winter, 1953.

Contains "Scholiast." Collected in *Like I Say.*

29. The Poetry Book Magazine, Vol. 5, No. 3. Brooklyn, New York, Spring, 1953.

Contains "A Country Without Ruins." Uncollected.

30. Variegation. Los Angeles, Calif., Summer, 1956.

Edited by Grover Jacoby. Contains "Tell Me More," and "A New Voyage." Uncollected.

31. The Cambridge Review #6. Cambridge, Mass., Fall, 1956.

Contains "Invocation: To the Muse," and "If You're So Smart, Why Ain't You Rich?" Both poems collected in *Like I Say.*

32. Coastlines 6, Vol. 2, No. 2. Los Angeles, Calif., Coastlines, Winter, 1956.

Edited by Mel Weisburd. Contains "The Engineer." Collected in *The Calendar: A Book of Poems.*

33. Ark II, Moby I. San Francisco, Calif., Spring, 1957.

Edited by Michael McClure and James Harmon. Contains "Martyrdom of Two Pagans." Collected in *A Casebook on the Beat.*

34. Evergreen Review, Vol. 1, No. 2. New York, N.Y.., Grove Press, Inc., April, 1957.

Edited by Barney Rosset and Donald Allen. Contains "The Road-Runner" (*Like I Say*); "Homage to Robert Creeley" (*Like I Say*); "Homage to Lucretius" (Uncollected); "Small Tantric Sermon" (*Like I Say*), and "Out of It" (Uncollected). The photograph of Philip Whalen is by Harry Redl.

35. Variegation. Los Angeles, Calif., Summer, 1957.

Edited by Mildred Okano. Contains "Unfinished, from 3:XII:55." Collected in *Like I Say.*

36. Ark III. San Francisco, Calif. [Dated Winter, 1957, released in January, 1958.]

Edited by James Harmon. Contains "A Dim View of Berkeley in the Spring." Uncollected.

37. The Black Mountain Review 7. Black Mountain, North Carolina, The Black Mountain Review [Dated, Autumn, 1957, released early in 1958].

Edited by Robert Creeley. Contains "3 Variations: All About Love." Parts I and III of this poem were collected in *Like I Say*. Part II has not been collected.

38. Yugen 1. New York, N.Y., Yugen, Spring, 1958.

Edited by LeRoi Jones and Hettie Cohen. Contains "Further Notice," "Takeout, 4:II:58," and "Takeout, 15:IV:57." All three poems were collected in *Like I Say;* the middle poem as "4:2:59 Take I."

39. Chicago Review, Vol. 12, No. 1. Chicago, Ill., Chicago Review, Spring, 1958.

Edited by Paul Carroll. Contains "10:X:57, Forty-Five Years Since the Fall of the Ch'ing Dynasty." Collected in *Like I Say.*

40. Chicago Review, Vol. 12, No. 2. Chicago, Ill., Chicago Review, Summer, 1958.

Edited by Paul Carroll. Contains "Excerpt: Sourdough Mountain Lookout." Collected in the unabridged form in *Like I Say*. The abridged form was collected in *A Casebook on the Beat.*

41. Evergreen Review, Vol. 2, No. 5. New York, N.Y., Grove Press, Inc., July, 1958.

Edited by Barney Rosset and Donald Allen. Contains "For C." Collected in *Like I Say.*

81

42. Yugen 3. New York, N.Y., Yugen, 1958.

Edited by LeRoi Jones and Hettie Cohen. Contains "Soufflé." Collected in *Like I Say*.

43. Berkeley Bussei. Berkeley, Calif., Berkeley Bussei, Summer, 1958.

Contains "Scholiast." Collected in *Like I Say*.

44. Chicago Review, Vol. 12, No. 3. Chicago, Ill., Chicago Review, Autumn, 1958.

Edited by Paul Carroll. Contains the prose text, "Prose Take 1:VI:57." Collected in *Beat: Eine Anthologie* in a shortened version.

45. Combustion. Toronto, Canada, Combustion, 1959.

Edited by Ray Souster. Contains "Self-Portrait, Sad." Collected in *Memoirs of an Interglacial Age*.

46. Yugen 5. New York, N.Y., Yugen, 1959.

Edited by LeRoi Jones and Hettie Cohen. Contains "I returned to San Francisco." Collected in *Memoirs of an Interglacial Age*.

47. Evergreen Review, Vol. 3, No. 9. New York, N.Y., Grove Press, Inc., Summer, 1959.

Edited by Barney Rosset. Contains *Two Poems:* "Fond Farewell to the *Chicago Review*," and "Take, 25:III:59." Both poems were collected in *Braincandy*.*

48. Beatitude 4. San Francisco, Calif., John Kelley, Summer, 1959.

Edited by John Kelley. Contains "Re-take of 28:XII:57." Collected in *Beatitude Anthology*.

49. Jabberwock. Edinburgh, Scotland, Edinburgh University Review, 1959.

Edited by Alex Neish. Contains "Delights of Winter at the Shore." Collected in *Memoirs of an Interglacial Age*.

50. Foot, No. 1. San Francisco, Calif., Foot, n.d. [September, 1959].

Edited by Richard Duerden. Contains "Delights of Winter at the Shore." Collected in *Memoirs of an Interglacial Age*.

51. Beatitude #9. San Francisco, Calif., Bread and Wine Mission, September 18, 1959.

Edited by Pierre Delattre. Contains "Sourdough Mountain Lookout." Collected in *Like I Say*.

52. Vigil: New Writing by New Writers, Vol. 1, No. 2. Chicago, Ill., Roosevelt University, Autumn, 1959.

Edited by Arnold L. Kaye and R. R. Cuscaden. Contains "Something Nice About Myself." Collected in *Memoirs of an Interglacial Age*.
*Braincandy will be the title of Philip Whalen's next volume of poetry, to be published by The Poet's Press, New York, N.Y., in 1967.

53. Beatitude #12. San Francisco, Calif., Bread and Wine Mission, December, 1959.

Edited by Pierre Delattre. Contains "Notes 20:VII:58, in Which I Renounce the Notion of All Social Responsibility." Collected in *Memoirs of an Interglacial Age.*

54. The Galley Sail Review, No. 5 . . . LI PO Issue, Vol. 2, No. 1, San Francisco, Calif., The Galley Sail Review, Winter, 1959-1960.

Edited by Stanley McNail and Guest Editor, David Rafael Wang. Contains "Hymnus Ad Patrem Sinensis." Collected in *Memoirs of an Interglacial Age.*

55. Sidewalk, Vol. 1, No. 1. Edinburgh, Scotland, Sidewalk, n.d. [1960].

Edited by Alex Neish. Contains "With Compliments to E. H." Collected in *Memoirs of an Interglacial Age.*

56. Between Worlds; An International Magazine of Creativity, Vol. 1, No. 1, Denver, Colorado, Inter-American University, Summer, 1960.

Edited by Dr. Gilbert Neiman. Contains "I Am King Giant Dragon Sun Fading." Collected in *Braincandy.*

57. Evergreen Review, Vol. 4, No. 14. New York, N.Y., Evergreen Review, September-October, 1960.

Edited by Barney Rosset. Contains "The Same Old Jazz." Collected in *Like I Say.*

58. Beatitude #17. San Francisco, Calif., City Lights Books, October-November, 1960.

Edited by Lawrence Ferlinghetti. Contains "For My Father," "Me," and "I Give Up." Collected in *Braincandy.*

59. Yugen 7. New York, N.Y., Totem Press, 1961.

Edited by LeRoi Jones. Contains "Literary Life in the Golden West," "Sincerity Shot, 23:III:58," and "A Manuscript in Several Hands, 3:III:60." The latter poem is uncollected; the first two poems were collected in *Braincandy.*

60. Nomad 9. Culver City, Calif., Nomad, Summer, 1961.

Edited by Donald Factor and Anthony Linick. Contains *Three Poems:* "Esprit D'Escalier Rant, To A Departing Audience," "I Give Up," and "The First Day Of November." All three poems were collected in *Braincandy.*

61. The Floating Bear #9. New York, N.Y., The Floating Bear, 1961.

Edited by LeRoi Jones and Diane Di Prima. Contains "Itchy." Collected in *Braincandy.*

62. Rhinozeros. Munich, Germany, Rhinozeros, Summer, 1961.

Edited by Rolfe-Gunter Dienst. Contains an untitled letter-poem. Uncollected.

63. The Floating Bear #14. New York, N.Y., The Floating Bear, 1961.

Edited by LeRoi Jones and Diane Di Prima. Contains "Goodbye & Hello, Again, 6:II:60." Uncollected.

64. Origin 4. (Second Series.) San Francisco, Calif., Origin, January, 1962.

Edited by Cid Corman. Contains "Address to a Younger Generation," "Real San Francisco Sunday Afternoon," and "Short Explanation of Everything." All three poems were collected in *Braincandy*.

65. Evergreen Review, Vol. 6, No. 24. New York, N.Y., Evergreen Review, Inc., May-June, 1962.

Edited by Barney Rosset. Contains "Historical Disquisitions." Collected in *Braincandy*.

66. Foot. San Francisco, Calif., Foot, Fall, 1962.

Edited by Richard Duerden and William Brown. Contains "The Death of Boston," and "Homage to Rodin." Both poems are uncollected. The *Doodles* on the inside front and back covers are by Philip Whalen, with those on the inside back cover being collected in *Highgrade*.

67. Outburst 2. London, England, The Matrix Press, 1963.

Edited by Tom Raworth. Contains "Irregular Ode, to Mlle K." Collected in *Braincandy*.

68. Now. San Francisco, Calif., Now, 1963.

Edited by Charles Plymell. Contains "One Page Poem." Collected in *Highgrade*.

69. The Desert Review, Penny Poetry Sheet No. 4. Albuquerque, New Mexico, The Desert Review Press, 1963.

Edited by Ward Abbott and Bryant Cashion. Contains "World Out of Control." Collected in *Braincandy*.

70. The San Francisco Chronicle, April 8, 1963.

Contains "Reality Sandwiches From Foster's," a book review of Allen Ginsberg's *Reality Sandwiches*.

71. The Floating Bear #27. New York, N.Y., The Floating Bear, 1963.

Edited by Diane Di Prima. Contains *The Art of Literature* (a group of 17 poems). Collected in *Braincandy*.

72. Fuck You / A Magazine of the Arts, Vol. 4, No. 5. New York, N.Y., Ed Sanders, n.d. [1963].

Edited by Ed Sanders. Contains "Duerden Says: Life Is Therapy." Uncollected.

73. Mithrander. San Francisco, Calif., Mithrander, n.d. [1963].

Edited by Tony Sherrod. Contains "A Vision of the Bodhisattvas." Collected in *Braincandy*.

74. Change. San Francisco, Calif., Change, 1963.

Edited by Ron Loewinsohn and Richard Brautigan. Contains "Spring Poem to the Memory of Jane Ellen Harrison (1850-1928)." Collected in *Braincandy*.

75. The Rivoli Review, Vol. 1, No. 1, San Francisco, Calif., The Rivoli Review, 1963.

Edited by Richard Duerden. Contains "Plums, Metaphysics, an Investigation, a Visit and a Short Funeral Ode in Memory of William Carlos Williams." Collected in *Braincandy*.

76. Northwest Review, Vol. 6, No. 4. Eugene, Oregon, University of Oregon Student Publications Board, Fall, 1963.

Edited by Edward van Aelstyn. Contains "Minor Moralia," "Tennis Shoes," "The Chariot," "One of My Favorite Songs Is Stormy Weather," "Friday Already Half—;" "A Short History of the Second Millennium B.C.," "Monday, in the Evening, 21:VIII:61," "PW His Recantation." The poem of the same name was collected in *Monday, In the Evening, 21:VIII:61*. The remaining poems were collected in *Braincandy*.

77. Genesis West, Vol. 2, No. 5. Burlingame, Calif., The Chrysalis West Foundation, Fall, 1963.

Edited by Gordon Lish. Contains "Warnings, Responses, Etc." Collected in *Braincandy*.

78. The San Francisco Chronicle, October 13, 1963.

Contains "Creeley Wants to Make Himself Clear," a book review of Robert Creeley's, *The Island*.

79. Ferret, Vol. II, No. 6. n.p. [Oakland, Calif.], [California College of Arts and Crafts Student Publication], October 16, 1963.

Contains "How Beautiful." Collected in *Braincandy*.

80. Open Space #3. n.p. [San Francisco, Calif.], Open Space, n.d. [1964].

Edited by Stan Persky. Contains "Technicalities for Jack Spicer." Collected in *Braincandy*.

81. New Student Review No. 9. Buffalo, New York, State University of New York at Buffalo, 1964.

Edited by William Cuddihy. Contains "Salamander." Collected in *Braincandy*.

82. The Desert Review. Albuquerque, New Mexico, The Desert Review Press, 1964.

Edited by Ward Abbott and Bryant Cashion. Contains "To the Muse." Collected in *Braincandy*.

83. Wild Dog, Vol. 1, No. 8. Pocatello, Idaho, Wild Dog, May, 1964.

Edited by Drew Wagnon. Contains "Twin Peaks," "Saturday Morning," "The Prophecy," "Oh Yes. Vancouver," and "The Fourth of October, 1963." All collected in *Braincandy*.

84. Poetry Review #2. Tampa, Florida, University of Tampa, August, 1964.

Edited by Duane Locke, R. Morris Newton, W. T. Cuddihy, and Paul Babikow. Contains "Letter to Michael McClure, 11:III:63." Collected in *Braincandy*.

85. Fuck You / A Magazine of the Arts, Vol. 7, No. 5. New York, N.Y., Ed Sanders, August, 1964.

Edited by Ed Sanders. Contains "Statement of Condition," "The Great Beyond Denver," "Papyrus Catalogue," "Vector Analysis," Against the Magic War: an Open Letter to Robert Duncan." All collected in *Braincandy*.

86. New Student Review No. 10. Buffalo, New York, State University of New York, State University of New York at Buffalo, 1964.

Edited by William Cuddihy. Contains "Vancouver." Collected in *Braincandy*.

87. Lines #2. New York, N.Y., Lines, December, 1964.

Edited by Aram Saroyan. Contains "Delusions of Reference." This poem became one of the sections in the poem, "The Best of It," which was collected in *Every Day*.

88. Evergreen Review, Vol. 8, No. 34. New York, N.Y., Evergreen Review, Inc., December, 1964.

Edited by Barney Rosset. Contains "For a Picture by Mike Nathan." Collected in *Braincandy*.

89. Synapse 3. Berkeley, Calif., Synapse, January, 1965.

Edited by D. R. Hazelton. Contains "Essex Was a Cowboy in Vermont," "A Mistake," and "St. Francis Lobbies Allen G." All collected in *Braincandy*.

90. Tri-Quarterly. Evanston, Illinois, Northwestern University, Winter, 1965.

Contains "The Season." Collected in *Braincandy*.

91. Upriver; Currents of Poetry, Vol. I, No. 111. Philadelphia, Pennsylvania, Winter, 1965.

Edited by Norman Weinstein. Contains "Illness," and "Some Kind of Theory." Collected in *Braincandy*.

92. Lines #3. New York, N.Y., Lines, February, 1965.

Edited by Aram Saroyan. Contains "The Best of It." Collected in *Every Day*.

93. *C*, a Journal of Poetry, Vol. I, No. 10. New York, N.Y., *C*, February 14, 1965.

Edited by Ted Berrigan. Contains "The Ode to Music." Collected in *Every Day*.

94. Intrepid, 1st Anniversary Issue, No. 5. New York, N.Y., Allen De Loach, March, 1965.

Edited by Allen De Loach. Contains "The Treasures of Rage," "Song for 2 Balalaikas on the Corner of 3rd & Market," and "Social Graces." All collected in *Braincandy*.

95. The San Francisco Observer, Vol. I, No. 4. San Francisco, Calif., April 8, 1965.

Contains "The Chain of Lakes." Collected in *Every Day*.

96. The Grande Ronde Review #2. La Grande, Oregon, The Grande Ronde Review, Spring, 1965.

Edited by Michael Andrews. Contains "Life and Death and a Letter to My Mother Beyond Them Both." Collected in *Braincandy*.

97. Poetry, Vol. 106, Nos. 1-2. Chicago, Ill., Poetry, April-May, 1965.

Edited by Henry Rago. Contains "Invocation and Theophany." Collected in *Braincandy*.

98. Lines #5. New York, N.Y., Lines, May, 1965.

Edited by Aram Saroyan. Contains an untitled reproduction of a page in the poet's handwriting. Collected in *Highgrade*.

99. Synapse #4. Berkeley, Calif., Synapse, May, 1965.

Edited by D. R. Hazelton. Contains "Brueghel: 'The Fall of Icarus' 20:IX:63," and "EAMD." Both collected in *Braincandy*.

100. Wild Dog #17. San Francisco, Calif., Wild Dog, June 8, 1965.

Edited by Drew Wagnon, Gino Clays, and Joanne Kyger. Contains "Fragment of Great Beauty & Stillness," "Doukhobor Proverb," "Disgust with a Poetical Evening at Miss Q's House," and "GRAND HISTORICAL ODE, to a Certain LADY Who Has Praised My Poems." All uncollected.

101. Vietnam Blues. San Francisco, Calif., Robert Peterson, 1965.

> Edited by Robert Peterson. Contains "Dear Mr. President." Previously published as a poster.

102. Now Now. San Francisco, Calif., Ari Publications, 1965.

> Edited by Charles Plymell. Contains "Mexico," "Corinthian Columns," "March 1964," "ABC," and "Treasures of Heaven." "ABC" was collected in *Highgrade*. The remaining poems were collected in *Every Day*.

103. The Paris Review, Vol. 9, No. 34. Paris, France, The Paris Review, Spring-Summer, 1965.

> Edited by Thomas Clark. Contains "To the Muse." Collected in *Braincandy*.

104. Things #2. New York, N.Y., The Association for the Promotion of Contemporary Literature and Art, Summer, 1965.

> Edited by Emmett Jarrett and Ron Schreiber. Contains "Somebody Else's Aesthetic." Collected in *Braincandy*.

105. Fux Magascene. San Francisco, Calif., Ari Publications, 1965.

> Edited by Robert R. Branaman. Contains "Movie Night," "San Francisco Sunday Morning Palimpsest," "Spring Musick," and "Native Speech." All collected in *Braincandy*.

106. Now Now Now. n.p. [San Francisco, Calif.], Now Now Now, n.d. [1965].

> Edited by Charles Plymell. Contains "Homage to William Seward Burrough." Uncollected.

107. Blitz. La Grande, Oregon, Blitz / Madvirgin Press, n.d. [1965].

> Edited by Bobby Watson and Mel Buffington. Contains "Re-Take 20:XII:63 from 7:III:63," collected in *Braincandy*, and "Trinity Sunday 1964," uncollected.

108. Spero. Flint, Michigan, Fenian Head Centre Press, 1965.

> Edited by Douglas Casement. Contains "To a Poet," and "To the Moon." Both collected in *Braincandy*. The trade edition of this magazine was issued in white wrappers, with 100 numbered copies of the *Contributor's Edition* in brown wrappers.

109. Intrepid, First Anniversary Issue / March 1964-March 1965. New York, N.Y., Intrepid Press, March, 1965.

> Edited by Allen De Loach. Contains "The Treasures of Rage," "Song for 2 Balalaikas on the Corner of 3rd & Market," and "Social Graces."

110. Or #1. Boulder Creek, Calif., Or, April, 1965.

> Edited by David Sandberg. Contains "Art and Society," "Temporarily Insane," "Farewell!," and "Song to Begin *Rohatsu*."

111. A New Folder; Americans: Poems and Drawings, edited by Daisy Aldan, with a foreword by Wallace Fowlie. New York, N.Y., Folder Editions, August, 1959.

1000 copies only, of which 850 were bound in stiff paper boards, and the remaining 150 in cloth over boards in dust jacket. Contains "Metaphysical Insomnia Jazz," collected in *Memoirs of an Interglacial Age*.

112. Helgon & Hetsporrar; Poesi fran Beat Generation och San Franciscorenassansen, edited by Reidar Ekner. Stockholm, Sweden, Raben & Sjogren, 1960.

Decorative wrappers. Contains "Liten tantrisk predikan" (*Small Tantric Sermon*, collected in *Like I Say*), "Tagning 25:III:59" (*Take-out 25:III:59*, collected in *Braincandy*), "Homage à Robert Creeley" (collected in *Like I Say*), and "Utanfor" (*Out of It*, collected in *Braincandy*).

113. The Beat Scene, photographs by Fred McDarrah, edited and with an introduction by Elias Wilentz. New York, N.Y., Corinth Books, distributed by The Citadel Press, 1960.

Pictorial wrappers. Contains "Sauced," collected in *Braincandy*. A photograph of Whalen appears on the facing page.

114. The New American Poetry: 1945-1960, edited by Donald M. Allen. New York, N.Y., Grove Press, Inc., 1960.

Clothbound in dust jacket, and in decorative wrappers [two editions]. Contains "Martyrdom of Two Pagans," "2 Variations: All About Love," "Sourdough Mountain Lookout," "Denunciation: or, Unfrock'd Again," "The Same Old Jazz," "Forty-Five Years Since the Fall of the Ch'ing Dynasty," "For C.," "Take I, 4:II:58." The lead poem is uncollected, the others appear in *Like I Say*. Whalen has also contributed a statement on poetics, p. 420, which is reprinted from *Memoirs of an Interglacial Age*.

115. Beatitude Anthology, edited by Lawrence Ferlinghetti. San Francisco, Calif., City Lights Books, 1960.

Pictorial wrappers. Contains "Retake of 28:XII:57," which is to be collected as "I Think of Mountains," in *Braincandy*.

116. A Casebook on the Beat, edited by Thomas Parkinson. New York, N.Y., Thomas Y. Crowell Company, 1961.

Decorative wrappers. Contains "Excerpt: Sourdough Mountain Lookout," collected in its unabridged form in *Like I Say*, "A Dim View of Berkeley in the Spring," collected in *Braincandy*, "For C.," collected in *Like I Say*, and "Martyrdom of Two Pagans," only book appearance.

117. JUNGE AMERIKANISCHE LYRIK, edited by Gregory Corso and Walter Hollerer. Munich, Germany, Carl Hanser, 1961.

> Wrappers in slipcase, with 45 rpm record inserted. Contains in bilingual text: "The Slop Barrel; Slices of the Paeiduma for All Sentient Beings." Both poems are from *Like I Say*.

118. BEAT: Eine Anthologie, herausgegeben von Karl O. Paetel. Reinbek bei Hamburg, Germany, Rowohlt Verlag, November, 1962.

> Decorative wrappers. Contains "Fur C." (*For C.*), "Prosa Aufnahme 1:VI:57" (*Prose Take 1:VI:57*). Both are from *Like I Say*.

119. 'BEAT' POETS, selected by Gene Baro. London, England, Vista Books / The Pocket Poets, Longacre Press Limited, 1961.

> Wrappers. Contains " 'Plus Ca Change . . .' " (unauthorized cut version of the first eleven lines only. The complete poem appears in *Like I Say*), and "Fond Farewell to the *Chicago Review*," collected in *Braincandy*.

120. POESIA DEGLI ULTIMI AMERICANI, a cura di Fernanda Pivano. Milano, Italy, Le Comete 35, Feltrinelli Editore, November, 1964.

> Pictorial wrappers. Bilingual text on facing pages. Contains "Homage to Rodin," to be collected in *Braincandy*, and "I Return to San Francisco," from *Memoirs of an Interglacial Age*.

PHONOGRAPH RECORDS

121. SAN FRANCISCO POETS. Evergreen Records, Lp, No. EVR-1, New York, 1957. Contains booklet of poems recorded and photos of the poets. (Now distributed by Hanover Records, New York.)

> Philip Whalen reads three of his poems: "The Road Runner," "Homage to Robert Creeley," and "Small Tantric Sermon."

122. JAZZ CANTO: An Anthology of Poetry and Jazz, Vol 1. World Pacific Records, Lp, No. WP-1244, Hollywood, Calif., December, 1958.

> Philip Whalen's poem, "Big High Song for Somebody" is read by Roy Glenn, with jazz background by the Gerry Mulligan quartet.

TAPE RECORDINGS

Philip Whalen has made tape recordings of his work for the Library of Congress and the following colleges and universities: San Francisco State College; The Poetry Room of Lamont Library, Harvard University, Cambridge, Mass.; Goddard College Library, Plainfield, Vermont; and the University of California, Berkeley.

CRITICISM

The Saturday Review, Vol. XL, No. 47. New York, N.Y., Saturday Review, Inc., November 23, 1957.

Page 32 contains the article, "Writers as Readers of Poetry," by John Ciardi, which includes a review of *San Francisco Poets* (Evergreen Records).

San Francisco Examiner, Highlight section, Sunday, October 5, 1958.

Page 17 contains "Kerouac as the Savant of the Religious Beat" (a review of *The Dharma Bums*), by Luther Nichols. Philip Whalen is given significant mention and is pictured with Kerouac, Allen Ginsberg, and Gregory Corso, in the photograph that accompanies the review.

Big Table 4. Chicago, Ill., Big Table, Inc., 1960.

Edited by Paul Carroll. Pages 128-132 contain "Writing for the Ear," by Paul Blackburn, a review of *San Francisco Poets* (Hanover Records).

San Francisco Examiner, Sunday, October 2, 1960.

Page 8 contains the article, "The Spiritual Quest of Poets Who Are Witty and Serious," by Thomas Parkinson. Included is a review of *Like I Say*.

Poetry, Vol. 97, No. 2. Chicago, Ill., Poetry, November, 1960.

Edited by Henry Rago. Pages 114-120 contain the article, "A Poetry Chronicle," by Henry Birnbaum, which contains a review of *Memoirs of an Interglacial Age*.

Kulchur 3. New York, N.Y., Kulchur Press Inc., 1961.

Edited by Marc Schleifer. Pages 79-81 contain reviews of *Like I Say* and *Memoirs of an Interglacial Age*, by Gilbert Sorrentino.

Yugen 7. New York, N.Y., Totem Press, 1961.

Edited by LeRoi Jones. Pages 13-18 contain the article, "The New World," by Robert Creeley, in which *Self-Portrait From Another Direction* is reviewed.

The New York Times Book Review, Vol. LXVII, No. 36. New York, N.Y., The New York Times Company, September 9, 1962.

Pages 5, 34 contain the article by Jack Gilbert, "Between Verses: Report on a West Coast Poetry Festival." Philip Whalen is given significant mention and is pictured in a photograph that accompanies the article.

The Oregon Journal. Portland, Oregon, Friday, June 5, 1964.

Contains the article, "Merits of Poetry Disputed; Role of UO Review Defended," by Jim Long, in which the editor of *Northwest Review* is assailed for printing Philip Whalen and Antonin Artaud.

The Oregon Journal. Portland, Oregon, Monday, June 8, 1964.
Contains the article, "UO Poems Held Not Obscene."

San Francisco Chronicle, Sunday Bonanza, July 11, 1965.
Edited by Theodore L. Bredt. Pages 16-17 contain, "Hike the Tenderfoot Trail," by Margot Patterson Doss, with photos by Dargent Calli. Article about hiking with Philip Whalen, with a photograph of the poet on page 16.

Work / 2. Detroit, Michigan, Artist's Workshop Press, Fall, 1965.
Edited by John Sinclair. Pages 108-115 contain reviews of *Monday, in the Evening, 21:VIII:61*, and *Every Day*, by Robin Eichele.

Holiday, Vol. 39, No. 3. Philadelphia, Pa., The Curtis Publishing Company, March, 1966.
Edited by Don A. Schanche. Pages 147-151 contain the article by Kenneth Rexroth, "A Hope for Poetry." Whalen is given significant mention.

DAVID MELTZER

David Meltzer

DAVID MELTZER is a young man of nervous and restless energy who bounds along on narrow, dirty white tennis shoes that seem capable at any moment of giving their author flight, as if they had been poetized into believing, along with their owner, that terrestrial well-being is deservant of celestial bliss. His hair is combed in an impermanent uncomb that appears to be an inverted, unbrushed wig, while his dress is a form of impermanent undress in that one can not imagine there ever having been the man nonconnective with the clothing; as if the particular time were the eternal moment. His clothing achieves the height of his neck in sweaters and jackets in a series of wrappings that are more bundle than attire, and even his neck is invisible because of an indoor-outdoor scarf that seems to give ballast to an airborne being. But the only skin visible has changed, has, in fact, been shed layer by layer until its present state is of an almost luminous white, which is more a spiritual state than a physical color. The eyes are otter-brown, and where they were once troubled, uneasy, and concealed the opposite of pity, they are now otter-brown in quietude and poise.

Meltzer has taken his religious vows and can not say, as he once did, that writing forms a part of his life, not all of it. What he does say now is that he is not to be judged by his previous work. He has a new responsibility to his writing that is based, one suspects — by viewing the poet as a man — upon the kind of courage that has become a faith.

Two years ago, about the time of our first meeting, David went from poetry to music (he didn't quit one for the other, he didn't stop writing poetry and start playing guitar, he merely *went* from poetry to music). He recently returned. I didn't know at the time that he was a poet, perhaps he himself did not know. He didn't talk personally as a man, but of opinions and ideas, and if he was, as it seemed, interested in everything then everything, presumably, was not enough. He seemed negative and pessimistic. The humor was too often clever, even facile, and the smile was that of the curled lip. He would nihilate his throat with smoke, one cigarette after another, always gesturing, always on the move, or he would sit down in a heap, arms and legs crossed, thinking: then leap upward like a spastic puppet jerked forward by the strings of his idea. He was full of life but of a kind that must perish (by nervous exhaustion and negative re-turns) to give birth to the real, the second life — the first culminating in consciousness — the second beginning with understanding and pity.

On the strings of his music he was taking one final exotic flight into fantasy; the voyage was from himself, but inside himself, and now that he has circled the globe of his mind he has come home at last. He made the connective link between hope and actuality, between what a man had hoped for for himself and for all humanity, and what indeed was possible. He could only know, he could only make a beginning by submitting, by assuming a stance that would comprise a life — that of the poet. To want everything is to have nothing. To accept the limitation of one's time and talent is the highest courage, for thereafter one can no longer make the excuse of not knowing oneself. One's ugliness, one's despair are now known. *All* may no longer be possible, but something *has* come to bear the stamp of man's effort and agony. He *is* responsible. He doesn't know but he is not ashamed of this confession. This much, he says, one word shaped from the clay of insubstance. Here, I sign my name, that I may assume the grief and shame.

David still plays Bluegrass guitar and sings publicly with his wife, billing themselves, DAVID AND TINA. The music, he says, is something. It's fun, a diversion he can share with other people, but it is not something he must feel responsible for.

Poetry? He's taken his vows. It's everything.

96

FRONT COVER, NO. 3, TITLE PAGE, NO. 5

BOOKS & BROADSIDES

1a. POEMS (with Donald Schenker). San Francisco, Calif., n.d. [1957].

Printed wrappers. Privately printed by Donald and Alice Schenker. 500 copies only, of which

1b. 5 numbered copies, with separate colophon, in paper boards signed and stained by the blood of the poets, and

1c. 25 copies, with separate colophon, in paper boards bound by hand [roughly divided among the poets, who created their own board designs] and numbered and signed by the authors.

1d. 15 copies of POEMS by David Meltzer comprising only the Meltzer section of the book, with a variant wrapper similar with the trade edition, but with the omission of Donald Schenker's name.

2. RAGAS. San Francisco, Calif., Discovery Books, 1959.

Decorative tan wrappers. Cover design by Peter Le Blanc. About 1500 copies only.

3. THE CLOWN. Larkspur, Calif., Wallace Berman (Semina VI), 1960.

Pictorial wrappers. 335 copies only.

4. WE ALL HAVE SOMETHING TO SAY TO EACH OTHER: Being An Essay Entitled Patchen And Four Poems. San Francisco, Calif., The Auerhahn Press, 1962.

Pictorial wrappers. In the photograph on the cover, Jennifer Love Meltzer, the poet's daughter. Auerhahn Pamphlet No. 2. 750 copies only.

5. BAZASCOPE MOTHER. Los Angeles, Calif., Drekfesser Press, n.d. [1964].

Folded broadside. The author's copy does not carry the pictorial credits, which are stamped on the front cover. About 500 copies only, of which less than 200 were distributed as give-away items; the remainder being destroyed by the publisher.

6.   STATION. n.p. [San Francisco, Calif.], East Wind Print-
     ers (A Poetry Folio, 1964.), 1964.

     Broadside. Collage by Peter Bailey. 300 copies. Created for the San
     Francisco Arts Festival 1964. A series of 10 broadsides by as many
     poets, with each broadside having a different illustrator. The colo-
     phon for the set is on a separate sheet, and with the 10 broadsides
     is laid loose in a golden-brown wrapper with a fuchsia title label.

7a. THE BLACKEST ROSE. n.p. [Berkeley, Calif.], Oyez, n.d.
     [1964].

     Broadside. 350 copies only. Printed by The Auerhahn Press for Oyez.
     No. 6 in the publisher's series of 10 broadsides.

7b. 27 copies of each broadside in the series were later signed by the ten
     poets and laid in a heavy linen board folder for separate sale. Only
     25 of these sets, which were prepared in 1965, were offered for sale.

8a. THE PROCESS. Berkeley, Calif., Oyez, 1965.

     Pictorial wrappers. Cover designs by Peter Le Blanc. Designed by
     Dave Haselwood. 500 copies. Illustrated with drawings by the author.

8b. 25 clothbound copies numbered and signed by the author, with dust
     jacket identical with wrapper covers.

8c. 5 copies, each individually bound in different board materials by
     Dorothy Hawley, with wrappers bound in, to celebrate the books
     going out of print. Prepared in January, 1967. Each copy separately
     decorated by the author and with a hand written colophon by him
     and signed by author, publisher, and binder.

EPHEMERA

9.   THE AUERHAHN PRESS CATALOG 1962. San Francisco,
     Calif., Auerhahn Press, 1962.

     Dark blue decorative wrappers. Contains the poem, "Self-Portrait"
     which was used to advertise the author's forthcoming book, *We All
     Have Something To Say To Each Other*. Collected in *The Process*.

10. OYEZ! n.p. [Berkeley, Calif.], Oyez, December, 1965.

     Folded broadside. Christmas card poem, 9-2/8 × 5-6/8 inches. The
     illustration in black on the front cover is by the poet and appears
     beneath the title, as above, which is in red. Printed on white rag
     paper. About 150 copies only.

PERIODICAL CONTRIBUTIONS

[All contributions are poems unless otherwise noted.]

11. Peninsula. Gainesville, Florida, University of Florida,
     1956.

     Contains "4 July," by Lionel (David) Meltzer. Uncollected. Only
     750 copies of this periodical were printed.

100

12. Semina 1. Los Angeles, Calif., Wallace Berman, n.d. [1956?].

Edited by Wallace Berman. Contains "An Unpublished Letter To Some Lost Relatives." Uncollected. All contributions loosely inserted on individual cards. Edition limited to 150 copies.

13. Dazzle. San Francisco, Calif., Playgirl Publishing Co., Inc., 1957.

Contains the short story, "Kick Me Deadly." Uncollected.

14. Semina Two. San Francisco, Calif., Wallace Berman, n.d. [1957].

Edited by Wallace Berman. Contains "Upon a Time." Uncollected.

15. Semina 4. San Francisco, Calif., Wallace Berman, 1959.

Edited by Wallace Berman. Contains "Sampson Agonistes." Uncollected. "Type handset on beat 5 × 8 Excelsior handpress." Edition limited to between 250-300 copies, many incomplete.

16. Spree, Vol. 1, No. 7. Los Angeles, Calif., New Publishing Company, Inc., 1959.

Contains the short story, "Judgement Day." Uncollected.

17. Beatitude #5. San Francisco, Calif., John Kelley, June 6, 1959.

Edited by John Kelley. Contains "It comes to this." Uncollected.

18. Beatitude #8. San Francisco, Calif., Bread and Wine Mission, August 15, 1959.

Edited by Pierre Delattre. Contains "18th Raga/ Fall," and "Prayer-wheel/ 2 — for John Weiners." Both poems were collected in *Beatitude Anthology.*

19. Penny Poems No. 27. New Haven, Conn., Penny Poems, 1959.

Broadsheet. Contains "24th Raga/ For Tina." Collected in *Ragas.*

20. Penny Poems No. 35. New Haven, Conn., Penny Poems, 1959.

Broadsheet. Contains "April" and "Two Poems for Joseph Matthew Loewinsohn, Age: 4 Months, 9 Days." Both collected in *Ragas.*

21. Penny Poems No. 54. New Haven, Conn., Penny Poems, 1959.

Broadsheet. Contains "The Prophet." Collected in *Ragas.*

22. Penny Poems No. 69. New Haven, Conn., Penny Poems, 1959.

Broadsheet. Contains "From: The Clown, Book II/ Air & Interim." Uncollected.

23. Penny Poems No. 83. New Haven, Conn., Penny Poems, 1959.

Broadsheet. Contains "Morning Poem." Uncollected.

24. The White Dove Review, Vol. 1, No. 3. Tulsa, Oklahoma, 1959.

Contains "(From: *The Disciple*)," "I Believe," "Satori," "Look Down & Watch," and "For the Poet: VII." All uncollected.

25. Yugen 5. New York, N.Y., LeRoi Jones and Hettie Cohen, 1959.

Edited by LeRoi Jones. Contains "15th Raga/ for Bela Lugosi" from "Night Before Morning/ Book One." Collected in *Ragas* as "15th Raga/ for Bela Lugosi."

26. Beatitude #9. San Francisco, Calif., Bread and Wine Mission, September 18, 1959.

Edited by Pierre Delattre. Contains "Song For Mother & Child: 2." Uncollected.

27. Beatitude #10. San Francisco, Calif., Bread and Wine Mission, October, 1959.

Edited by Pierre Delattre. Contains "After Hours," "Songs for Mother & Child: 1," and "From: Notes For A History." "After Hours" was collected in *Beatitude Anthology*. The other two are uncollected.

28. Beatitude #11. San Francisco, Calif., Bread and Wine Mission, November 2, 1959.

Edited by Pierre Delattre. Contains "The Faerie God Mother Earth —Angry," and "From: Notes for a History . . ." Both uncollected.

29. Beatitude #12. San Francisco, Calif., Bread and Wine Mission, December, 1959.

Edited by Pierre Delattre. Contains "From: Notes For A History." Uncollected.

30. Beatitude #13. San Francisco, Calif., Bread and Wine Mission, February, 1960.

Edited by Pierre Delattre and Associates. Contains "Bunko/ Letter II." Uncollected.

31. Big Table 4. Chicago, Ill., Big Table, 1960.

Edited by Paul Carroll. Contains "Notes For A History." Uncollected.

32. Beatitude #14. San Francisco, Calif., Bread and Wine Mission, May 6, 1960.

Edited by Pierre Delattre. Contains "Words/ October 7th." Uncollected.

33. Semina 5. n.p. [San Francisco, Calif.], Wallace Berman, n.d. [1960].

Edited by Wallace Berman. Contains "Todos santos. Villa." Uncollected. All contributions inserted loose on varying paper stock.

34. Beatitude #17. San Francisco, Calif., 1960.

Edited by Lawrence Ferlinghetti. Contains "Ride." Uncollected.

35. Yugen 6. New York, N.Y., LeRoi Jones and Hettie Cohen, 1960.

Edited by LeRoi Jones. Contains "4th Raga/ for John Kelley Reed." Uncollected.

36. The Galley Sail Review 7, Vol. 2, Nos. 3-4. San Francisco, Calif., The Galley Sail Review, Winter, 1960.

Contains "From the Prickbook of Rosy Thorne" and "Poem." Both uncollected.

37. Big Table, Vol. 2, No. 5. Chicago, Ill., Big Table, 1960.

Edited by Paul Carroll. Contains "Rain Poem," collected in *The Process*, and "Heroes: Zap, the Zen Monk," uncollected.

38. Renaissance, Vol. 1, No. 1. San Francisco, Calif., Renaissance Publications, 1961.

Edited by John Bryan and Michael O'Donoghue. Contains "How It's Done." Uncollected.

39. Rhinozeros. Germany, 1961.

Edited by Rolf-Gunter Dienst. Contains "Song." Uncollected.

40. Showcase, No. 4. Los Angeles, Calif., American Art Agency, 1961.

Contains the short story, "And all that Jazz." Uncollected. Also contained is a photograph of Meltzer.

41. Journal For The Protection of All Beings. San Francisco, Calif., City Lights Books, 1961.

Edited by Michael McClure, Lawrence Ferlinghetti, and David Meltzer. Contains the essay, "Journal of the Birth." Uncollected.

42. Renaissance, Vol. 1, No. 2. San Francisco, Calif., Renaissance Publications, 1962.

Edited by Stanley McNail. Contains "Beautiful beautiful beautiful." Uncollected.

43. The Floating Bear #18. New York, N.Y., Diane Di Prima and LeRoi Jones, 1962.

Edited by the publishers. Contains "Poem to H. P. Lovecraft," and "The Struggle/ Poems for Muse," and "Heroes: 7/ The Comics." All uncollected.

44. Renaissance, Vol. 1, No. 3. San Francisco, Calif., Renaissance Publications, 1962.

Edited by Stanley McNail. Contains "Young Girl on a Bus." Uncollected.

45. The Yale Literary Magazine, Vol. CXXXI, Nos. 3 & 4. New Haven, Conn., Yale Literary Society, April, 1963.

Edited by Michael G. Gill. Contains "Song of Death Singing." Uncollected.

46. Signal: A Quarterly Review, Vol. I, No. 1. New York, N.Y., Brownstone Press, Inc., 1963.

Edited by Bret Rohmer. Contains "Moon Poem." Uncollected.

47. Notes From Underground. San Francisco, Calif., Underground Press, 1964.

Edited by John Bryan. Contains "Love Poem." Uncollected.

48. Poetry Review, No. 3. Tampa, Florida, University of Tampa, 1964.

Contains "Youth Ritual Movie," "Rain Poems," and "Ride Out: 1956." All revised and collected in *The Process*.

49. Coyote's Journal #1. Eugene, Oregon, Coyote's Journal, 1964.

Edited by James Koller, Edward van Aelstyn, and William Wroth. Contains "Earth Quake," and "Station." Both collected in *The Process*. Author's name erroneously omitted in the table of contents.

50. Kulchur 17. New York, N.Y., Kulchur Press, 1965.

Edited by Lita Hornick. Contains two book reviews by Meltzer: *The Erasers*, by Alain Robbe-Grillet, and *Meet My Maker the Mad Molecule*, by J. P. Donleavy.

51. Synapse 4, San Francisco Issue. Berkeley, Calif., Synapse, May, 1965.

Edited by D. R. Hazelton. Contains "The Bath." Uncollected.

52. Coyote's Journal #4. Eugene, Oregon, Coyote's Journal, 1965.

Edited by James Koller, Edward van Aelstyn, and William Wroth. Contains "Chthonic Fragments," collected in *The Process*, and "Metaphors: —," uncollected.

53. Kulchur 20. New York, N.Y., Kulchur Press, Inc., Winter, 1965-1966.

Edited by Lita Hornick. Contains a book review by Meltzer of Henry Miller's, *The Rosy Crucifixion (Sexus, Nexus, Plexus)*.

104

54. THE NEW AMERICAN POETRY: 1945-1960, edited by Donald M. Allen. New York, N.Y., Grove Press, Inc., 1960.

   Clothbound in dust jacket, and in decorative wrappers [two editions]. Contains "Revelation," "12th Raga/ for John Weiners," and "15th Raga/ for Bela Lugosi," from *Ragas*, and "Prayerwheel/ 2."

55. BEATITUDE ANTHOLOGY, edited by Lawrence Ferlinghetti. San Francisco, Calif., City Lights Books, 1960.

   Pictorial wrappers. Contains "18th Raga/ Fall," "Prayerwheel/ 2— for John Weiners," and "After Hours."

56. JUNGE AMERIKANISCHE LYRIK, edited by Gregory Corso and Walter Hollerer. Munich, Germany, Carl Hanser, 1961.

   Wrappers in slipcase, with 45 rpm record inserted. Contains "15th Raga" and "Prayerwheel/ 2," from *Ragas*.

57. THE REAL BOHEMIA, by Francis J. Rigney and L. Douglas Smith. New York, N.Y., Basic Books, Inc., 1961.

   Pictorial wrappers. Contains "23rd Raga/ for Tina," "14th Raga/ for Donald Schenker," and "30th/ June: 59," from *Ragas*.

58. THE OUTSIDERS (Roman Books Catalogue Number Three). Fort Lauderdale, Florida, 1962.

   Wrappers. 750 copies only. Contains the Introduction by Meltzer.

CRITICISM

Mainstream, Vol. II, No. 7. New York, N.Y., Masses & Mainstream, Inc., July, 1958.

   Edited by Charles Humboldt. Page 14 contains a brief review of *Poems*.

Poetry, Vol. 96, No. 3. Chicago, Ill., Poetry, June, 1960.

   Edited by Henry Rago. Pages 179-185 contain "The Angels of Discombooberation," by Felix Stefanile, which includes a review of *Ragas*.

Kulchur, Vol. 3, No. 9. New York, N.Y., Kulchur Press, Inc., Spring, 1963.

   Edited by Gilbert Sorrentino. Pages 69-82 contain "Poetry Chronicle," by Gilbert Sorrentino, which includes a review of *We All Have Something to Say to Each Other*.

DAVID MELTZER: A Sketch from Memory and Descriptive Checklist, by David Kherdian. Berkeley, Calif., Oyez, April, 1965.

   Brown printed wrappers. Frontispiece drawing by Peter Le Blanc. 500 copies only. Designed and printed by Graham Mackintosh.

The National Observer, Vol. 4, No. 32. Silver Spring, Maryland, Dow Jones & Company, Inc., Monday, August 16, 1965.

Page 19 contains "Poetry 1965: Pleasant Rhymes to Bleeding Words," by Douglas M. Davis, which includes a review of *The Process*.

Kulchur, Vol. 5, No. 20. New York, N.Y., Kulchur Press, Inc., Winter, 1965-1966.

Edited by Lita Hornick. Contains a review of *The Process*, by George Bowering.

MICHAEL McCLURE

Michael McClure

MICHAEL McCLURE IS THAT RARITY, a writer who invites the reader to seek *pleasure* as the antidote to depression and ennui. He believes we are warm-blooded sensory creatures whose personal revelations lie in understanding and gratifying this "spiritmeat" or body-and-mind. This new concept of self-involvement has begun with the *Ghost Tantras*, which are exercises in learning, in becoming the man unafraid of the personal totalities of his spiritmeat. His enemy here is repression and the unconscious; and his intention is for the making of a new romantic: *mammal*. For McClure the old notion of *man* is no longer pleasing. The sensory images of his poetry concern the creatures with which he aligns himself because of their "warm-bloodedness": the falcon, eagle, and gyrfalcon; and the warm tempered salmon and kraken. To become, he feels, we must dare to become: man is not a cool cat, he is a warm-blooded-loving-balling-ape-mammal-bird-beast-fish. He must push out to the extreme limits of his being if he is to be free, unconquered, and capable of his own conquest and release. For McClure there can be no distinction between the man and the writer — one being condemned to serve the other — nor can there be a differentiation between the mind and the body; for if the mind is in error it will be reflected by a gesture of the body. The poise he is concerned with in the stance he strikes is determined by the position and balance of the mind: a man's walk being determined by the movement of his thought.

It is this fusion of mind and body as a single principle that is the particular stamp of the man, and it is this concept that has determined the flow of his work, which is of constant change, growth, and expansion. Unfortunately, the growing social concern of his poetry has entailed work in areas that no longer require a lyric quality, which is his finest poetic gift. The concept that determined *Ghost Tantras*, for example, could have been compressed into one poem, but to convey the idea with the force it required—if it were to have the impact on the public he intended—an entire book of poems had to be published.

McClure's best performances are often those in which he yields to a creative urge, and in the mysterious process of creation produces a work of which the eventual meanings can only be half-known to the artist. Outwardly, his Billy the

109

Kid, Jean Harlow plays appear as casual Pop Art performances in which the hero and heroine are displayed and allowed to prance and strike familiar poses. There is an objectivity here, however, that saves McClure; for while these two are truly his folk-heroes he is never unaware of their psychic disorders—which are the disorders of an entire civilization that lives in sexual catatonia—who, unable to live joyously and sensually with their bodies, erect heroes who are so psychically corrupted they are actually able to caricaturize what they can not do. McClure has the courage to write of the disease with the personality of one who is infected, but who wishes to cure and be cured. The aim of McClure is to undo and destroy, to kill the childhood daemons that haunt his adult life; even though in so doing the art he creates can only be transitory: even though he must kill his own heroes. To achieve an understanding and with this knowledge to transform thinking is what is needed—for it is only by being free of the myth of America that one can begin to understand the truth of this country. It is this awareness, this growing concern of contemporary values and concerns, that has broadened McClure's art and sharpened his ability to communicate—often in new forms—for the danger, as he well knows, is that we are losing one another and that only by direct and personal communication—even if only one hand reaching out to touch another—can art arrest and heal. There is no longer time for gentility and tradition in literature. The poet can not afford to talk from inside closed walls, either of the work room or the flesh; he must be willing to expose and dare all. This new awareness and responsibility has demanded new forms. For Bill Wilson, who is reluctant to publish, a new form of letter writing to friends: for the artist, Ray Johnson, who rarely exhibits, envelope-sized collages mailed to a circulating library of correspondents, and for Michael McClure, anonymous greeting cards with personal inscriptions, such as his exquisite and strikingly beautiful *Fuck Death* card.

Michael McClure is young and handsome, with brown wavy hair that runs down his neck and stops just teasingly short of his shoulders. His face tapers gently from a broad handsome forehead to a delicate chin. His eyes seem to carry one expression, which is a cross between glint and gleam, and together with his hands and feet are continuously busy: his feet, always within plain black Spanish boots; his hands never still, never exactly in gesture, are almost never without a

110

cigarette, almost a sixth finger—straight and lean—that counterbalance thick, fleshy hands. His dress is stylized: either a mustard-yellow cardigan sweater buttoned from top to bottom, or a suit coat and tie with the collar turned up. His pants: black denim; his boots: black high tops. His work is individual and changing, his dress individual and rigid: the purposeful design of a man obsessed with his image and role. For McClure it is this dividing of the juices between creativity and performance that have so often given his work the facility that is easy to respond to but also easy to forget. The indispensable legerdemain in performing for a fickle public is constant production, constant change — to anticipate and guide, to control and lead. This passion for swift and easy production occasionally finds McClure walking so furiously within the circle of his own talent he sometimes seems in danger of colliding with himself.

Our first meeting took place in Berkeley at the Oyez publishing offices when I turned in the manuscript of my monograph on David Meltzer, and McClure had stopped by to see the advance sheets of his play, *The Beard*. He knew of my intention to do a prose sketch and checklist on him and he was eager to talk and learn of my intentions and the point of view I was establishing for the series. We chatted about the Midwest, where we were both born and raised — about the rain and snow, the smells and sounds, and how they differed from California. More than anything he seemed to remember and miss the icy chill of winter that remained in the shoulders on into spring, and he came to understand that this became the symbol of remembrance and longing for him. The conversation moved on to new forms in painting, the pleasure of living in San Francisco (and that, as he said, the so-called *San Francisco Poets* were only those individuals who wanted to write poetry and to do so in the best city in America — San Francisco; and he couldn't understand why this was given a group-movement label). Before going to lunch we went out to put money in our parking meters, my car a Volkswagen, Mike's a red Triumph. Walking back upstairs I remarked that no matter how long one owns a Volkswagen it remains totally and miserably unchanged, at no moment taking on the properties of the owner. He agreed excitedly and told me of the Volkswagen he had owned before his present car and how, after two years, he had given it up as hopeless. Later, the four of us, Robert Hawley, Oyez publisher; Graham Mackintosh, free-lance printer; McClure and I, went to lunch. Earlier Mike and I had discussed the school where he teaches English and Drama. He had begun what he termed Chance Drama in which the dialogue for the play, in the present case, *The Last Christian,* was written on individual cards as poems by the members of the class. The students would take roles and perform the parts with their own decks or exchanging decks. The movement and meaning in the play would be determined by the ability of the students to make their lines enter into the plot and design of the drama. McClure felt that such improvisatory exercises would be liberating for his students and would allow a further range of expression than in normal drama. After lunch, walking back four abreast, McClure, rather than return upstairs with the rest of us as I had expected, suddenly flanked-off and was, when I looked up, halfway across the street turning three-quarters with a wave of farewell with one hand, the other in the front pocket of his black denims. By the time we reached the office door he was already part way down the street in his ground-hugging red sportscar — and with his collar upturned and his hair brushing his shoulders, it didn't seem impossible that he *would* change reality (for himself) — and possibly for others.

BOOKS, BROADSIDES, POSTERS

1. PASSAGE. Big Sur, Calif., Jonathan Williams, Jargon 20, June, 1956.

   Blue-gray printed wrappers. 200 copies only.

2. PEYOTE POEM. n.p. [San Francisco, Calif.], Wallace Berman (Semina 3), n.d. [1959].

   Folded broadside encased in brown pictorial wrappers. About 200 copies. Not for sale.

3. FOR ARTAUD. New York, N.Y., The Totem Press (Blue Plate #2), June, 1959.

   White decorative wrappers. 750 copies only.

4. HYMNS TO ST. GERYON AND OTHER POEMS. San Francisco, Calif., The Auerhahn Press, October, 1959.

   Tan decorative wrappers. Cover design from a silk screen by the author. 950 copies only. Designed by Dave L. Haselwood.

5a. !THE FEAST! San Francisco, Calif., The Batman Gallery, 1960.

   Mimeographed working script of the play produced at The Batman Gallery, December 22, 1960. Not for sale.

5b. Mimeographed press release announcing the play as *A Titan Mystery Play in One Act*, which contains a line in beast language, presumably by McClure.

6. THE NEW BOOK/ A BOOK OF TORTURE. New York, N.Y., Grove Press (Evergreen Original E-306), August, 1961.

   Decorative wrappers. 4000 copies only. Published simultaneously in London by Evergreen Books Ltd. See also No. 19.

7. PILLOW. New York, N.Y., New York Poets Theatre, 1961.

   Photocopied from the original typescript for use as a working script for the performance of the play by the New York Poets Theatre at the Off-Bowery Gallery, New York City, in 1961. Not for sale.

115

8a. DARK BROWN. San Francisco, Calif. The Auerhahn Press, 1961.

Dark brown printed wrappers. 750 copies only, of which

8b. 25 copies bound in red-brown leatherette binding for subscribers, signed by the author.

9. MEAT SCIENCE ESSAYS. San Francisco, Calif., City Lights Books, July, 1963.

Decorative wrappers. 3000 copies only. Photo of McClure on inside front cover by Ettore Sotsass.

10a. TWO FOR BRUCE CONNER. n.p. [Berkeley, Calif.], Oyez, 1964.

Broadside. 450 copies only. Printed by The Auerhahn Press for Oyez. No. 1 in the publisher's series of 10 broadsides.

10b. 27 copies of each broadside in the series were later signed by the poets and laid in a heavy linen board folder for separate sale. Only 25 of these sets, which were prepared in 1965, were offered for sale.

11a. GHOST TANTRAS. San Francisco, Calif., Michael McClure, 1964.

Pictorial wrappers. 1500 copies only, of which

11b. 20 copies numbered and signed by the author, bound in black cloth over boards, dust jacket same as regular issue wrappers, with the same text rearranged to fit on flaps and back cover. Certificate of issue page tipped in after page [2]. A copy of BLUE-BLACK ... [No. 24] inserted loose.

12a. THE BLOSSOM: OR BILLY THE KID. New York, N.Y., American Theatre for Poets, Inc., June, 1964.

Mimeographed working script for the actors and for distribution to interested persons. Page 27 is misnumbered. Not for sale. See also No. 23.

12b. A 3-minute 16mm film of scenes from this production was made by George Herms.

13a. LOVE LION, LIONESS. n.p. [Berkeley, Calif.], [Oyez], n.d. [December 10, 1964].

Fight poster, 28½ x 22⅛ inches. Lettered in red and blue with photo portraits of William H. Bonney and Jean Harlow, with their names beneath, with virtually all of the lettering in beast language. 350 copies only, of which 100 were placed for sale.

13b. 5 sets, numbered and signed, not for sale.

13c. Issued with each poster were two fight tickets written in beast language. A total of 700 copies (2 tickets per poster) were printed.

116

14. THIRTEEN MAD SONNETS. Milano, Italy, East 128 Milano [1965].

Yellow-orange printed wrappers. Photographs of the author by Ettore Sottsass, Jr. Number 5 in the publisher's series, *Autori scelti da Fernanda Pivano.* 315 copies only, of which 299 have been numbered and placed for sale. Printed by serigraphy in the author's holograph. Publication date was erroneously given as 1964, the proposed date of publication.

15. THE BEARD. n.p. [Berkeley, Calif.], [Oyez], n.d. [April, 1965].

Pictorial wrappers. 350 copies. Designed by the author and privately distributed to actors and friends, except for 75 copies which were placed for sale by the publisher. See also Nos. 28 and 29.

16a. POISONED WHEAT. San Francisco, Calif. [Oyez], 1965.

Pictorial wrappers. 576 copies privately published for the author as a give-away item.

16b. 24 signed copies lettered in the Greek alphabet bound in maroon linen over boards. Placed for sale.

17. UNTO CAESAR, by anonymous. n.p. [San Francisco, Calif.], [Dave Haselwood], n.d. [June, 1965].

Decorative wrappers. Hand stitched and printed from hand-set type. Each page contains a one-line poem. Published without a title page. 100 copies only, of which 10 copies were placed for sale.

FUGITIVE PIECES & EPHEMERA

18. THE AUERHAHN PRESS [Catalog]. San Francisco, Calif., The Auerhahn Press, n.d. [1959].

Folded broadside tipped into tan wrappers, 7-13/16 scant x 5-2/8 inches. A small number were issued without the wrapper. Contains "Oh Christ God Love Cry of Love Stifled Furred Wall Smoking Burning." Collected in *A New Book/A Book of Torture.*

19. From *The New Book / A Book of Torture.* Cambridge, Mass., Paterson Society, 1961.

8vo. printed sheet. Contains a statement by the poet. Not otherwise printed.

20. GRAHHR . . . n.p. [San Francisco, Calif.], [The Auerhahn Press], n.d. [1963].

Small sheet containing one-line poem. About 200 copies. Not for sale.

21. SPACE GRACE . . . n.p. [San Francisco, Calif.], [The Auerhahn Press], n.d. [1964].

Small sheet containing one-line poem. About 200 copies. Not for sale.

22. POETRY IS A MUSCULAR PRINCIPLE . . . n.p. [Los Angeles, Calif.], [Wallace Berman], n.d. [May, 1964].

Pictorial card, 8-17/32 x 5-19/32 inches. Announcement of a reading by the author, containing a statement on poetry. Photograph of the author, nude, with beast make-up, by Wallace Berman is reproduced four times across the card. This photograph, cropped, to show head only, appears as the front cover illustration for *Ghost Tantras*. Not for sale.

23. THE BLOSSOM OR BILLY THE KID. n.p. [New York, N.Y.], The American Theatre for Poets, Inc., n.d. [1964].

Mimeographed program for performance of the play by the American Arts Project. Contains "Let Us All Be Drunk on Music!"

24. BLUE-BLACK . . . n.p. [San Francisco, Calif.], [The Auerhahn Press], n.d. [1964].

Small sheet containing one-line poem. About 200 copies. Not for sale.

25. DOUBLE MURDER: VAHROOOOOOOHR! n.p. [Los Angeles, Calif.], [Wallace Berman, Semina 9], 1964.

Stiff white card, 2-31/32 x 4-6/8 inches. Contains a single poem, inserted loose in a manila envelope which bears an altered photograph of Jack Ruby on the point of murdering Lee Harvey Oswald. Not for sale.

26. FUCK DEATH. n.p. [San Francisco, Calif.], [Michael McClure], n.d. [1964].

Folded greeting card. Unlettered throughout except for the front cover which contains a blue-gray horse's head with a silver horseshoe directly above on which the title is lettered in black. Privately printed and personally inscribed as a give-away item to friends. Printed by Dave Haselwood in an edition of about 100 copies.

27. BLOT RAINBOW FLASH!!! n.p. n.d. [New York, N.Y., June 5, 1965]

Dummy newspaper, 22-6/8 x 16-9/16. Printed as a headline. Privately printed in an edition of 7 copies.

28. INVITATION TO PREMIERE PERFORMANCE OF *The Beard*. n.p. [San Francisco, Calif.], [Dave Haselwood], n.d. [December, 1965].

Single fold cream colored invitational mailer, 3-15/16 x 6-1/2 inches. Lettering on inside covers only. Printed vertically in red on the two lettered pages is McClure's one word signature, GRAHHR.

29. THE SAN FRANCISCO ACTOR'S / WORKSHOP GUILD, INC./ presents / a preview of / MICHAEL McCLURE's / *The Beard*. n.p. n.d. [San Francisco, Calif., December, 1965].

Mimeographed sheet, 13-15/16 x 8-1/2 inches. Contains the essay, "Dressed in Meat and Flowered Shirt," and an untitled poem.

30a. DREAM TABLE. San Francisco, Calif., Dave Haselwood, January, 1966.

White pictorial card poem, 3-9/16 x 2-15/32 inches. 30 cards, consisting of the title on one card, author, publisher, site, and date on another card, and 28 cards with single words at each end of each card.

30b. Twenty signed sets comprised a limited edition.

31. The Poetry Center, March 23, 1966/MICHAEL McCLURE

8vo. mimeographed sheet. Contains AUTOBIOGRAPHICAL by McClure, which is reprinted from *A Controversy of Poets*. This is the first separate printing of this autobiographical note.

PERIODICAL CONTRIBUTIONS

[*All contributions are poems unless otherwise noted.*]

32. Poetry, Vol. 87, No. 4. Chicago, Ill., Poetry, January, 1956.

Edited by Henry Rago. Contains *2 for Theodore Roethke:* "Premonition" and "2." This is McClure's first appearance in print. Uncollected.

33. Ark II / Moby I. n.p. [San Francisco, Calif.], James Harmon, 1956-1957.

Edited by Michael McClure and James Harmon. Contains "Canoe: Explication," and "Logos: Knout." Collected in *'Beat' Poets*.

34. Combustion, Number Two. Toronto, Canada, Contact Press, April, 1957.

Contains "Fuseli." Uncollected.

35. Semina Two. n.p. [San Francisco, Calif.], Wallace Berman, n.d. [1957].

Contains "I Wanted to Turn to Electricity—I Needed." Collected in *Hymns to St. Geryon and Other Poems*.

36. Life, Vol. 43, No. 11. Chicago, Ill., Time, Inc., September 9, 1957.

Contains the first six lines of "The Robe." Collected in *Hymns to St. Geryon*.

37. Evergreen Review, Vol. I, No. 2. New York, N.Y., Grove Press, Inc., 1957.

Edited by Barney Rosset and Donald Allen. Contains "Night Words: The Ravishing," collected in *Passage* and *Hymns to St. Geryon;* "Cat's Air," uncollected; "The Rug," collected in *Hymns to St. Geryon;* "The Note," uncollected, and "The Robe," collected in *Hymns to St. Geryon*. Photo of McClure by Harry Redl.

119

38. Measure, No. 2. San Francisco, Calif., John Weiners, Winter, 1958.

Edited by John Weiners. Contains "The Magazine Cover," "One," and "Two." All uncollected.

39. Chicago Review, Vol. 12, No. 1. Chicago, Ill., Spring, 1958.

Contains "The Mess," "7/26/57," "Less Than Vanity," and "The Breech." The last poem was collected in *Hymns to St. Geryon;* the others are uncollected.

40. Black Mountain Review, No. 7. Black Mountain, North Carolina, Black Mountain College [Dated Autumn, 1957, released early in 1958].

Edited by Robert Creeley. Contains "Poem." Collected in *Passage,* and *Hymns to St. Geryon.*

41. Evergreen Review, Vol. II, No. 6. New York, N.Y., Grove Press, Inc., Autumn, 1958.

Edited by Barney Rosset and Donald Allen. Contains "Ode to Jackson Pollock." Collected in *The New Book / A Book of Torture.*

42. Jabberwock. Edinburgh, Scotland, Edinburgh University Review, 1959.

Edited by Alex Neish. Contains "For Artaud," "A Fantasy and Courtly Poem," and "Ode for Soft Voice." All three poems were collected in *The New Book / A Book of Torture.*

43. Beatitude 5. San Francisco, Calif., John Kelley, June 6, 1959.

Edited by John Kelley. Contains "Lines From a Peyote Depression." Collected in *The New Book / A Book of Torture,* and *Beatitude Anthology.*

44. Semina 4. San Francisco, Calif., Wallace Berman, 1959.

Edited by Wallace Berman. Contains "We're in the Middle of a Deep Cloud." Collected in *A New Book / A Book of Torture.* "Type hand-set on beat 5 x 8 Excelsior handpress." Edition limited to between 250-300 copies, many incomplete.

45. Yugen 4. New York, N.Y., Yugen, 1959.

Edited by LeRoi Jones. Contains "The Chamber." Uncollected. A two-line quote from this poem was used on the front cover of the magazine, *Trembling Lamb.*

46. The Galley Sail Review, Vol. 12, No. 1. San Francisco, Calif., Galley Sail Publications, Winter, 1959-1960.

Edited by Stanley McNail and guest editor, David Rafael Wang. Contains "L'Etoile." Collected in *The New Book / A Book of Torture.*

47. Sidewalk, Vol. I, No. 1. Edinburgh, Scotland, n.d. [1960].
1960.

Contains "The Flower of Politics." Collected in *The New Book / A Book of Torture*, and *The New American Poetry: 1945-1960*.

48. Big Table, Vol. I, No. 4. Chicago, Ill., Big Table, Spring, 1960.

Edited by Paul Carroll. Contains "Two Poems From a Small Secret Book." Collected in *The New Book / A Book of Torture*.

49. Yugen 6. New York, N.Y., LeRoi Jones and Hettie Cohen, 1960.

Edited by LeRoi Jones. Contains "The Column." Collected in *A New Book / A Book of Torture*.

50. Semina 5. n.p. [San Francisco, Calif.], Wallace Berman, n.d. [1960].

Edited by Wallace Berman. Contains "We Are Impervious as the Skin of Our Dreams." Uncollected. All contributions inserted loose on varying paper stock. 350 copies only.

51. Beatitude 17. San Francisco, Calif., City Lights Books, November, 1960.

Edited by Lawrence Ferlinghetti. Contains "Oh Why Oh Why the Blasted Love the Huge Shape Change? Oh Why." Collected in *Dark Brown*.

52. The Floating Bear #1. New York, N.Y., LeRoi Jones, February, 1961.

Edited by Diane De Prima and LeRoi Jones. Contains "The Smile Shall Not Be More Mutable Than the Final Extinction of Meat. The Smile." Uncollected.

53. Nomad 9. Los Angeles, Calif., Nomad, Summer, 1961.

Contains "To Kirby," "Billy the Bat," "Madrigal," "Marchons," "Blues," "The Answer," "Doble Guzano," "Ode to Sweety Bird." All uncollected.

54. Lunes De Revolucion. Havana, Cuba, n.d. [1961?].

Contains "La Brecha" [The Breech], and a brief quote from a letter by McClure, translated into Spanish.

55. The Floating Bear #14. New York, N.Y., LeRoi Jones, Fall, 1961.

Edited by Diane Di Prima and LeRoi Jones. Contains the play, "!The Feast!"

56. The Outsider, Vol. I, No. 1. New Orleans, La., Loujon Press, Fall, 1961.

Edited by Jon Edgar Webb. Contains "Spontaneous Hymn to Kundalini." Uncollected.

57. Evergreen Review, Vol. 5, No. 20. New York, N.Y., Evergreen Review, September-October, 1961.

Edited by Barney Rosset. Contains "On Seeing Through Shelley's Eyes the Medusa." Uncollected.

58. Journal for the Protection of All Beings. San Francisco, Calif., City Lights Books, 1961.

Edited by Lawrence Ferlinghetti, David Meltzer, and Michael McClure. Contains the essay, "Revolt." Collected in *Meat Science Essays*.

59. Kulchur, Vol. 2, No. 8. New York, N.Y., Kulchur Press Inc., Winter, 1962.

Edited by Marc D. Schleifer. Contains "Phi Upsilon Kappa." Uncollected.

60. Foot, No. 2. Berkeley, Calif., Foot Magazine, 1962.

Edited by Richard Duerden and William Brown. Contains "The Surge." Uncollected.

61. Pa'lante, No. 1. New York, N.Y., The League of Militant Poets, 1962.

Edited by Howard Schulman. Contains "Fidelio," and "Twigs." The latter poem is uncollected. "Fidelio" was collected in *Poets of Today*.

62. El Corno Emplumado / The Plumed Horn, No. 3. Mexico City, Mexico, Anaxagoras, July, 1962.

Edited by Margaret Randall and Harvey Wolin. Contains "Dear Jane," and "Drunk Writing." Both uncollected.

63. Origin 6. Kyoto, Japan, Origin, July, 1962.

Edited by Cid Corman. Contains "The Held Back Pain." Uncollected.

64. Evergreen Review, Vol. 6, No. 25. New York, N.Y., Evergreen Review, July-August, 1962.

Edited by Barney Rosset. Contains the essay "Drug Notes." Collected in *Meat Science Essays*.

65. Fuck You / A Magazine of the Arts, No. 4. New York, N.Y., Ed Sanders, August, 1962.

Contains "The Mind Pain Comes Over Me and I Am Blunked .." Uncollected.

66. The Nation, Vol. 196, No. 3. New York, N.Y., The Nation Company, January 19, 1963.

Contains "The Human Face." Uncollected.

67. The Outsider, Vol. 1, No. 3. New Orleans, La. Loujon Press, Spring, 1963.

Edited by John Edgar Webb. Contains "Three Mad Sonnets Nos. 6, 7, and 11." Nos. "6" and "11" were collected in *13 Mad Sonnets*. No. "7" was not collected.

122

68. Poetry, Vol. 102, No. 3. Chicago, Ill., Poetry, June, 1963.

Edited by Henry Rago. Contains "The Child," and "Two Mad Sonnets." Collected in *13 Mad Sonnets*.

69. Artforum, Vol. II, No. 1. San Francisco, Calif., July, 1963.

Contains "Dog Star Man—the first 16 millimeter epic." Reprinted in Film Culture, No. 29, Summer, 1963. Uncollected.

70. Semina 8. Los Angeles, Calif., Wallace Berman, 1963.

Contains "Ghost Tantra." Collected in *Ghost Tantras*.

71. City Lights Journal, No. 1. San Francisco, Calif., City Lights Books, 1963.

Edited by Lawrence Ferlinghetti. Contains "Notes on Miniature Drama." Uncollected.

72. Now. San Francisco, Calif., Charles Plymell, 1963.

Edited by Charles Plymell. Contains "Pompous Adolescent (beyond proper years), Vain," and "Black and Yellow Pansy." The first poem is uncollected; the latter was collected in *13 Mad Sonnets*.

73. Fuck You / A Magazine of the Arts, Vol. 4, No. 5. New York, N.Y., Ed Sanders, 1963.

Edited by Ed Sanders. Contains "Fuck Essay." Uncollected.

74. Northwest Review, Vol. 6, No. 4. Eugene, Oregon, University of Oregon Student Publications Board, 1963.

Edited by Edward van Aelstyn. Contains "Artaud: Peace Chief." Reprinted from *Meat Science Essays*.

75. Ferret, Vol. II, No. 6. n.p. [Oakland, Calif.] [California College of Arts and Crafts Student Publication], October 16, 1963.

Contains "Note." Uncollected.

76. Evergreen Review, Vol. 8, No. 32. New York, N.Y., Evergreen Review, April/May, 1964.

Edited by Barney Rosset. Contains the play "The Growl." Uncollected.

77. Joglars, Vol. 1, No. 1. Providence, R.I., Joglars, Spring, 1964.

Edited by Clark Coolidge and George Palmer. Contains "Stanza 13 from Love Lion Book." Uncollected.

78. Film Culture, No. 32. New York, N.Y., Film Culture, Spring, 1964.

Edited by Jonas Mekas. Contains "Defense of Jayne Mansfield." Uncollected.

79. Gnaoua, No. 1. Tangier, Morocco, Ira Cohen, Spring, 1964.

Contains "The Beast Sound: Nine Poems." Collected in *Ghost Tantras*.

80. Cleft, Vol. 1, No. 2. England, May, 1964.

Contains "Ghost Tantra 50." Collected in *Ghost Tantras*.

81. Kulchur, Vol. 4, No. 14. New York, N.Y., Kulchur Press, Inc., Summer, 1964.

Edited by Lita Hornick. Contains the essay "Reason." Uncollected.

82. Imago, No. 1. Calgary, Alberta, Canada, University of Alberto, 1964.

Edited by George Bowering. Contains "Three Poems from the Beast Sound." Collected in *Ghost Tantras*.

83. Fuck You / A Magazine of the Arts, Vol. 7, No. 5. New York, N.Y., Ed Sanders, September, 1964.

Edited by Ed Sanders. Contains "Airs from a Forgotten Book." [3 poems]. Uncollected.

84. Now Now. San Francisco, Calif., Charles Plymell, January, 1965.

Edited by Charles Plymell. Contains an offset reproduction of the poster *Love Lion, Lioness,* and the two tickets which accompany the poster. See Nos. 13a and 13c.

85. Dimas 3. February, 1965.

Contains "For Me," "For a Drawing by Bruce Conner," "Only Simplicity," "You—New to Me," and "The Convertible." Uncollected.

86. My Own Mag, No. 11. England, February, 1965.

Contains "Dream Tables" (Nos. 1 and 2).

87. The San Francisco Keeper's Voice, No. 2. San Francisco, Calif., Alexander Weiss, February, 1965.

Edited by Alexander Weiss. Contains "Ghost Tantra 15." Reprinted from *Ghost Tantras*.

88. Fuck You / A Magazine of the Arts, Vol. 8, No. 5. New York, N.Y., Ed Sanders, March, 1965.

Contains two letters to the editor, one of which contains an excerpt from *Poisoned Wheat,* and a series of poem cards reproduced in the poet's holograph.

89. C, a Journal of Poetry, Vol. I, No. 10. New York, N.Y., Ted Berrigan, February 14, 1965.

Contains "Ghost Tantra #9." Reprinted from *Ghost Tantras*.

90. Fux Magascean. San Francisco, Calif., Ari Publications, 1965.

Edited by Robert R. Branaman. Contains "Wondersmitten! Trance-like! Profound!" Uncollected.

91. Sigma Portfolio, No. 21. London, England, Alexander Trocchi, 1965.

Contains "Revolt." Reprinted from *Meat Science Essays*.

BOOK APPEARANCES

92. A New Folder; Americans: Poems and Drawings, edited by Daisy Aldan, with a foreword by Wallace Fowlie. New York, N.Y., Folder Editions, August, 1959.

1000 copies only, of which 850 were bound in stiff paper boards, and the remaining 150 in cloth over boards in dust jacket. Contains "The Chamber."

93. The Holy Barbarians, by Lawrence Lipton. New York, N.Y., Julian Messner, Inc., 1959.

Clothbound in dust jacket. Contains "Peyote Poem."

94. The Beat Scene, edited by Elias Wilentz. New York, N.Y., Corinth Books, 1960.

Wrappers. Photos by Fred McDarrah. Contains "Yes and Hands and Arms Yes Table Dark Squatty and Strong." Photo of McClure, p. 140.

95. Beatitude Anthology, edited by Lawrence Ferlinghetti. San Francisco, Calif., City Lights Books, 1960.

Wrappers. Contains "Lines from Peyote Depression."

96. The New American Poetry: 1945-1960, edited by Donald M. Allen. New York, N.Y., Grove Press, Inc., 1960.

Clothbound in dust jacket, and in decorative wrappers [two editions]. Contains "The Breech," "The Rug," "Hymn to St. Geryon, I," "Canticle," "Peyote Poem, Part I," "Ode for Soft Voice," "For Artaud," "The Flowers of Politics, I & II," and "From a Journal."

97. Helgon & Hetsporrar; Poesi fran Beat Generation och San Franciscorenassansen, edited by Reidar Ekner. Stockholm, Sweden, Raben & Sjogren, 1960.

Wrappers. Contains "Meskalinpoem."

98. Junge Amerikanische Lyrik, edited by Gregory Corso and Walter Hollerer. Munich, Germany, Carl Hanser, 1961.

Wrappers in slipcase, with 45 rpm record inserted. Contains in bilingual text: "Night Words," "The Ravishing," and "For the Death of 100 Whales."

99. TIGER, words selected by Lyle E. Linville, photographed by James C. Hansen. Cortland, Ohio. Linville-Hansen Associates, Inc., 1961.

Pictorial wrappers, spiral bound. Contains excerpts from three of McClures' poems, one of which serves as the book's epigraph.

100. MAXIMUS FROM DOGTOWN — 1, by Charles Olson. San Francisco, Calif., The Auerhahn Press, 1961.

Wrappers. 500 copies only. Contains a foreword by McClure.

101. 'BEAT' POETS, selected by Gene Baro. London, England, Vista Books / The Pocket Poets, Longacre Press Limited, 1961.

Wrappers. Contains "Canoe: Explication," and "Logos: Knout."

102. A CASEBOOK ON THE BEAT, edited by Thomas Parkinson. New York, N.Y., Thomas Y. Crowell Company, 1961.

Wrappers. Contains "Point Lobos: Animism," and "Peyote Poem."

103. POESI DEGLI ULTIMI AMERICANI, a cura di Fernanda Pivano. Milano, Italy, Le Comete 35, Feltrinelli Editore, November, 1964.

Wrappers. Bilingual text on facing pages with exceptions noted in brackets. Contains "Ghost Tantra 51," "The Column," "Fuck Ode" [English only], "Phi Upsilon Kappa" [Italian only], "A Garland" [English only].

104. POETS OF TODAY; a New American Anthology, edited by Walter Lowenfels. New York, N.Y., International Publishers, 1964.

Clothbound and in wrappers [two editions]. Contains "Fidelio."

105. LA POESIE DE LA BEAT GENERATION, translated by Jean-Jacques Lebel. Paris, France, Denoel, 1965.

Wrappers. Contains "Apres une Depression au Peyotl."

106. A CONTROVERSY OF POETS; an Anthology of Contemporary American Poetry, edited by Paris Leary and Robert Kelley. Garden City, N.Y., Doubleday & Co., Inc., Anchor Books, 1965.

Wrappers. Contains "Oh Ease Oh Body-Strain Oh Love Oh Ease Me Not! Wound Bore," "The Aelf-Acin, the Shining Scimmer the Gleam, the Shining," and "Oh Bright Oh Black Singbeast Loudbeast Catkin Sleek." Also contained is a biographical statement by McClure at the back of the book.

RECORDINGS

107. SAN FRANCISCO POETS. Evergreen Records, Lp, No. EVR-1, New York, 1957.

> Contains booklet of poems recorded and photos of the poets. (Now distributed by Hanover Records, New York.) Michael McClure reads four of his poems: "Night Words," "The Ravishing," "Cat's Air," and "The."

108. THE SULLEN ART. New York, Radio Station WBAI, 1961.

> Tape recorded interview with David Ossman, "The Sullen Art." [32 minutes.]

109. MAD SONNETS AND BEAST SOUNDS. Berkeley, Calif., Radio Station KPFA, 1963.

> Tape recording of reading by McClure. [42 minutes.]

110. POET MICHAEL McCLURE READING AT THE FLEISHACKER ZOO. San Francisco, Calif., recorded by Bruce Kansas Conner.

> Photo of McClure by W. Berman. Edition limited to 50 tapes, of which 6 tapes were numbered and signed by McClure and placed for sale.

CRITICISM

Life, Vol. 43, No. 11. Chicago, Ill., Time, Inc., September 9, 1957.

> Pages 105-109 contain the article, "Big Day for Bards at Bay." Photo.

The Saturday Review, Vol. XL, No. 47. New York, N.Y., Saturday Review, Inc., November 23, 1957.

> Page 32 contains "Writers as Readers of Poetry," a review by John Ciardi of San Francisco Poets (Evergreen Records).

Commentary, Vol. 24, No. 6. New York, N.Y., American Jewish Committee, December, 1957.

> Edited by Elliot E. Cohen. Pages 475-9 contain "America's 'Angry Young Men'; How Rebellious Are the San Francisco Rebels?," by Dan Jacobson.

America: National Catholic Weekly Review, Vol. CI, No. 26. Norwalk, Conn., America Press, September 26, 1959.

> Edited by Harold C. Gardiner. Pages 766-768 contain the article, "Those 'Beat' Writers," by Wolfgang B. Fleischmann.

Life, Vol. 47, No. 22. Chicago, Ill., Time, Inc., November 30, 1959.

> Pages 115-130 contain the article, "The Only Rebellion Around," by Paul O'Neil.

Big Table, Vol. I, No. 4. Chicago, Ill., Big Table, Inc., Spring, 1960.

Edited by Paul Carroll. Pages 124-126 contain "Notes on Young Poets," by Allen Ginsberg. Pages 128-132 contain "Writing for the Ear," by Paul Blackburn, a review of *San Francisco Poets* (Hanover Records).

Poetry, Vol. I, No. 4. Chicago, Ill., Poetry, November, 1960.

Edited by Henry Rago. Pages 114-120 contain the article, "A Poetry Chronicle," by Henry Birnbaum, which contains a review of *Hymns to St. Geryon*.

Kulchur 3. New York, N.Y., Kulchur Press, Inc., 1961.

Edited by Marc Schleifer. Pages 81-85 contain a review of *Hymns to St. Geryon*, by LeRoi Jones.

Yugen 7. New York, N.Y., Totem Press, 1961.

Edited by LeRoi Jones. Pages 13-18 contain "The New World," by Robert Creeley, in which *Hymns to St. Geryon and Other Poems* is reviewed.

Lunes De Revolucion. Havana, Cuba, n.d. [1961?].

Pages 5-6 contain the article, "Poetas a Caballo: Weiners y McClure."

Saturday Review, Vol. XLIV, No. 44. New York, N.Y., Saturday Review, Inc., November 4, 1961.

Page 26 contains a review of *The New Book / A Book of Torture*, by Malcolm Brinnin.

San Francisco Sunday Chronicle, This World, April 8, 1962.

Page 35 contains "A McClure Poem Would Turn Emily Into Smoke," a review of *The New Book / A Book of Torture*, by Jack Foss.

Poetry, Vol. C, No. 5. Chicago, Ill., Poetry, August, 1962.

Edited by Henry Rago. Pages 329-333 contain the article "Three Poets," by George Oppen, which includes a review of *Dark Brown*.

Kulchur, Vol. 2, No. 8. New York, N.Y., Kulchur Press, Inc., Winter, 1962.

Edited by Gilbert Sorrentino. Pages 89-91 contain a review of *The New Book / A Book of Torture*, by Edward Dorn.

MEAT SCIENCE ESSAYS, by Michael McClure. San Francisco, Calif., City Lights Books, July, 1963.

A note on MEAT SCIENCE ESSAYS, by Lawrence Ferlinghetti.

Frontier, Vol. 15, No. 2. Los Angeles, Calif., Frontier, December, 1963.

Edited by Phil Kerby. Pages 18-20 contain the article, "The Political Role of the Artist," by Lawrence Lipton, which is devoted almost entirely to the reviewing of *Meat Science Essays*.

Kulchur, Vol. 4, No. 13. New York, N.Y., Kulchur Press, Inc., Spring, 1964.

Edited by Lita Hornick. Contains a review of *Meat Science Essays*, by Jerome Rothenberg.

The Times Literary Supplement. London, England, Thursday, March 25, 1965.

Page 236 contains "This Is Geryon," a review of McClure's literary career to date by Eric Mottram.

Work/1. Detroit, Michigan, Artist's Workshop, Summer, 1965.

Edited by John Sinclair. Contains a review of *Ghost Tantras*, by Jerry Younkins.

Wild Dog #18. San Francisco, Calif., Wild Dog, July 17, 1965.

Edited by Drew Wagnon, Gino Clays, Joanne Kyger, and contributing editor, Ed Dorn. Contains a review of *Ghost Tantras*, by Richard Brautigan.

Fact, Vol. II, No. 4. New York, N.Y., Fact Magazine, Inc., July-August, 1965.

Edited by Warren Boroson. Page 40 contains "A Summer Reading List To End All Summer Reading Lists," by G. Legman, which contains a review of *Dark Brown*.

Work/2. Detroit, Michigan, Artist's Workshop Press, Fall, 1965.

Edited by John Sinclair. Pages 96-101 contain a review of *Thirteen Mad Sonnets*, by Jerry Younkins.

A Catalog of Works by Michael McClure 1956-1965, compiled by Marshall Clements. New York, N.Y., The Phoenix Book Shop, Inc., 1965.

Tan printed wrappers.

San Francisco Chronicle, Tuesday, December 21, 1965.

Page 39 contains "Folk Heroes in Old Rite," a review of the performed play, *The Beard*, by Michael Grieg. Photo.

BROTHER ANTONINUS

Brother Antoninus

Brother Antoninus lives in a Dominican Priory in Kentfield, California. It is a short drive from San Francisco and a pleasant one because of the scenery. One may take the highway that begins at the Golden Gate bridge and drive straight to the Kentfield turnoff, from which the priory is a short drive, or it is possible, although much slower, to avoid the highway almost all together by driving through the cities of Sausalito, Mill Valley, and Larkspur, striking Kentfield just north of the road on which the Dominican Prior is settled. The priory is not as large as one would expect, and it is a rather unassuming building except for the deliberate simplicity of its structure. The building is a white-wash stucco with brown trim and a brown shingled roof. Adjacent to the priory is a tennis court and one is surprised, at first, to learn that the players are Dominican Monks.

Brother Antoninus' cell is in the rear of the building and, because the downstairs is ground level, he has a level view of the grounds from the room's only window. A floor-to-ceiling bookcase runs the length of the right-hand wall, and the opposite wall of this small, oblong room is taken up by Brother Antoninus' bed and the wash basin. There are two chairs in the room but preferring the comfort of his bed, he usually sits, legs sprawled and with his back propped against the pillow. This was the position he took for the interview. Except for his white T shirt he was dressed entirely in black: denim trousers, stretch socks, and cardigan sweater. His black cordovan shoes had been removed.

His posture, his physicalness, so manifest his interior state that it is impossible to point to the revealing gesture or glance, for they all communicate his present condition. His face is gaunt; his hair, which is softly gray, is never combed except by his hands; his mouth, at moments of intense pain curls downward to form an elongated, inverted U, and even his body is elastic and can change instantly depending on how he stands within himself at a particular moment. In the middle of his speech he will suddenly murmur something almost inaudible of which he is barely aware and which sounds to the listener like an incantation of grief. His hands are in constant expression, no less when they are perfectly still than when they form a cup for his buried face. They form a variety of expressions when he is speaking: when animated by an exciting

133

idea that is suddenly emerging, as much to his amazement as to the listeners, he will sweep across with one hand at the moment of its culmination in a karate chop that means an idea has been finalized. This movement, in particular, is an insight into the most prevalent cadence of his poetry, for between lines one can almost hear the chop of finality. At other times, while an idea is slowly coming to light, he can gently and with feminine patience, coax it along with his fingers. When an unwanted word or two has found its way into the text of his speech he will slowly work his fingers back into that particular line of speech, as if it were a palpable text, and pull back the unwanted words as if they were attached to an invisible cord. In the same way he will insert a word or two that he has neglected, or that will lend power to his thought.

KHERDIAN: As a poet do you find that in the 20th Century the Church can still serve as muse? Hasn't the Church become too masculine and defensive for this to be possible any longer?

ANTONINUS: No, it's still possible. More so, in fact, than, say, a hundred years ago. There's been considerable recovery, largely unconscious, of the feminine spirit in Catholicism, as Jung pointed out regarding the recent Marian dogmas. I think in the Latin countries there was never any substantial loss. Certainly at the end of the Middle Ages the Church was everywhere the Great Mother—Holy Mother Church. It was with the uprush of erotic energies at the Renaissance that this feminine element began to transmute into another dimension and transform the entire culture. That great moment of radiance and ambience that was the Renaissance. The true feminization of culture in terms of poetry and art emerged then, together with all the social graces.

All that produced a wave of reaction, however, because of other, once powerful residual elements in the religion itself. Ascetic norms were being jettisoned in high places. The great wave of the Renaissance was followed by the great wave of the Reformation. There began the puritan attack to extirpate those feminine delicacies from the Great Mother and force all back on more ascetic norms, make her more "natural" in the Old Testament sense, by making her more simple. Simplicity and permanence, and to hell with art.

The revival of Old Testament patriarchial norms coincided with the rise of national states, the cult of kingship, the codification of Roman law, all severely masculine sensibility in the Baroque, but that was doomed by the triumph of rationalism, industrialism and, in the 19th Century, scientism. As for Catholicism, the commercial victory of Anglo Saxon and Teutonic Protestanism did put the Church on the defensive, and legalism and moralism carried the day. It was a bad time for the artist.

Being a bad time for the artists, they left the Church in droves. As a class, intellectuals generally did. With the capitulation of the intellectuals the new proletariat lost its natural ally, and it too fell away. The Church was left in the hands of the bourgeois. In the keeping of the middle class urban Catholicism inevitably became a conventionalized moralistic religion. Because the middle class doesn't have enough intellect [laughter] or enough vitality—it has neither the mind nor the instinct [peals of laughter] to sustain the true religious spirit. It can only conventionalize material existence, and it clings to the priesthood as father image, as security principle, the anxiety fixation of a rootless mercantile people. It is no life for the artist. They left in droves.

Now, however, with the breakdown of traditional middle class values and the recovery of authentic religious ones due to the universal crisis brought about by the double onslaught of two world wars, the breaking down, you might say, of both secularized middle class assumptions and proletarianized lower class ones (not to mention rationalized intellectual ones) shaken by two great wars hurled against their closed systems, and which will hurl again until those systems have utterly succumbed, we are forced, for better or for worse, toward a new, surely more open way of life, and in that just-glimpsed openness a new freedom promises.

Now, the return, at one level or another, by sensitive men to religious values, means that the more feminine side of Christianity, repressed since the Reformation, but retained in its sacramental deeps, is emerging. I do not refer to the Big Mother image projected almost superstitiously by so many elements of the lower classes, and by a certain sentimentalizing portion of the middle class itself. Rather the artist senses the recovery of his Muse in the Church by virtue of something else, the emergence up from her depths of the feminine instinct as Sophia, the Divine Wisdom. This spirit comes to us from the Old Testament. We find it in the Book of Wisdom

135

which the Protestant Bible excluded. But in the Vulgate the
Book of Wisdom manifests the Spirit under its feminine aspect.
It was so in ancient Jewish thought and it is so in the deeps
of the Catholic intuition. Listen:

> Wherefore I wished, and understanding was given me,
> and I called upon God, and the spirit of wisdom came
> upon me.

> And I preferred her before kingdoms and thrones, and
> esteemed riches nothing in comparison of her.

> Neither did I compare unto her any precious stone:
> for all gold in comparison of her, is as a little
> sand, and silver in respect to her shall be counted
> as clay.

> I loved her above health and beauty, and chose to have
> her instead of light: for her light cannot be put out.

> Now all good things came to me together with her, and
> innumerable riches through her hands.

> And I rejoiced in all these: for this wisdom went
> before me, and I knew not that she was the mother
> of them all.

> Which I have learned without guile, and communicate
> without envy, and her riches I hide not.

See what I mean? This is the Muse, pure and simple. And
she is splendid, the Bride of Christ. I have myself written
verses to her, which can't match those above, but again listen.
Not the whole poem but some stanzas out of the middle. I
have tried to get something of the passion, the instinct, which
make up the wisdom of life, the terror and the awe of the
Night of Nights.

> Savage and awesome as the birth of suns
> She treads a tumult on the stippling shore,
> Keeling the fleets of kings about her knees
> And drowning the sailors that her daughters bore.

> She is the Mother of Life, mistress of death,
> Before her feet the tiger coughs and dies.
> And the bony elephant gives up the boast
> Of those vast passions that once filmed his eyes.

> She is the Mother of Life, of Death the pride;
> Nothing in nature broke that Maidenhead.
> Man's glory entered life between her knees,
> Yet does she keep inviolable the Bed.

> Dung and all death are hers to keep and fend;
> The thirst of mules, the semen of the stag,
> Beat of the flesh and the flesh's diffidence,
> The sperm-swift cusped in the dreaming Bride.

136

When arrows beak the ridges of the bone
Hers is the hand; and when the widow weeps
Hers the invincible will that took the man,
Shovelling the dead up for her windrow heaps.

She is the Mother of Life, the Queen of Death,
Her only lover lives beyond the skies,
Coming to cover under the lightning flash—
The impregnation of the prophet's cry.

Upon a night of geysers by a sea
When the lost tribes stirred in their urgent dust,
And rain walked pelting through death's random slain
Stirring the whirling rapture of their lust,

She was accosted on a lonely hill
By what no man may guess, but in her womb
She bore the impact of the sacred Seed;
Her instinct broke the lordship of the Tomb.

Fire and passion, energy and source,
The blood's distemper and the mystic cry—
She met the wild lover face to face
And drank the hunger of the naked sky.

And so on. As Muse she holds it all, all life, it's all there. When
the poet speaks, when he finds his voice, it's Sophia, the wis-
dow, who is speaking through him.

KHERDIAN: If the Church is recovering her power as muse
for the poet, what of the crafts? You reached, I believe, the
apex of your career as a printer with the printing of the
Novum Psalterium PII XII, which is regarded by many to
be the finest book printed by an individual in this century.
Did you feel that you had gone as far as you could, or did
something happen in the printing of that book that made it
impossible for you to print again?

ANTONINUS: Something failed. Certainly the Church as muse
inspired that book, and certainly there was a breakdown, a
snapping of inspiration. I don't know. Maybe if we talk about
it we can find out why.

I began to get into printing after I'd reached a certain peak
in the writing of poetry. You generally struggle through life
to activate certain potentialities within yourself. You begin to
score early. You score by activating those potentialities and
finding your way into life, working your way into the col-
lectivity in terms of what you can do. I began as a poet. When
things opened up for me they came forth in a clear flow, pure

137

sensibility. Then ideas developed, and I had to labor in a craftsmanly way in order to explicate them, and the whole problem of formal exposition arose.

The first book of poems I did was, as I say, relatively easy, clear flowing, just right out of the unconscious. But with the beginning of *San Joaquin* I really had to start to labor, to perfect a craftsmanship in order to get those ideas across. This became more and more a developing thing as the war came on. I was impelled to struggle with that problem in my verse. And I was struggling through my life, writing it out as I was struggling, until the war ripped me out of the San Joaquin Valley, that great womb in which I'd been gestating, and I was thrown on the Oregon coast among ideationally motivated men, and other sides of my personality were forced to develop. Then came the failure of my marriage, and the great truncation and release brought a breakthrough in the writing of "Chronicle of Division." Not surprisingly, after that great pain had been worked through, had settled, it was as if craftsmanship itself had matured. I felt I had finally achieved a point from which I could engage ideas without struggling with craft. The craft began to be unconscious, at my fingertips, and it was at this point that I began to veer over toward another medium, the medium of printing.

I suppose it was inevitable that I should take up printing since my father had been a printer. I knew something of the atmospherics of printing from working around the shop as a boy, and it was natural that I should gravitate toward that mode of expression next. Initially I am inhibited by technique. It's the sensation side; that side of the psyche which has to do with concrete things—what Jung calls Sensation—this has always been my great limitation. I have always been impaired on that side (as well as on the side of more speculative processes like philosophy, mathematics, even arithmetic) so that I can only—I proceed only through techniques that have been fairly established in me by necessity, by the practice, experience, and requirements of life. And so it was natural that at Waldport when the group turned to printing, and I found others there to help me, that I should veer into printing and work out that potentiality within myself as a problem, as a life problem. I'm looking back on it now, but of course I didn't know these things at that time. You just go where you have to go, where life takes you.

As we worked on the press, and I gradually developed skill, I began to think in terms of the absolute typographical

138

achievement, which, I had heard, had come only from the handpress. As I have related elsewhere when I went to San Francisco on furlough I bought one and after the war I set that handpress up. I set about in a very determined way to master the craft finally and produce a book that was a consummate work of art. My idea was to write my poems, and then concretize them in a perfect format. To write a perfect poem, a perfect book of poems, and concretize it in a perfect format established on absolutely authentic materials. It was basically out of such motives that I launched into private printing.

Now you ask about the term of this process, the printing of the *Psalter*. That's partly compounded with my problem in the monastic life. By the time I'd done my second book on the handpress, *Triptych for the Living*, I was once again, from the craftsmanly point of view, approaching facility, just as I had painstakingly approached it in poetry. You struggle and struggle until you get what you want, but after a while the craft becomes natural to you and you don't have to struggle so much. You're not simply fighting to perfect a craft, but to reach a point where the craft becomes implicit, where the craft becomes unconscious. Until the craft enters into you, until the craft is memorialized in your very person, your very presence, you are not a master. When it achieves that point then you have the freedom of the craft and your genius, what you are, can manifest itself directly without equivocation.

I am known as a perfectionist in printing, and, I think it fair to say, an anti-perfectionist in poetry. I disclaim the distinction. It speaks more of the typographical and literary situation than it does of me. Actually there are printers so perfectionist that I have no interest in rivaling them. I was born under the sign of Virgo, but in the pursuit of perfection I know there is a point beyond which you cannot go, or "perfectionism" sets in. The norms of perfection begin to work against themselves. In either art I seek to approach that point, to achieve that point, but never to trespass beyond it. To go beyond it is worse, believe me, than to fail to reach it. What is still yet-to-be retains some of the power of the inchoate, the potential, whereas what is over-done is more than finished, it is finished off, "finalized"—the thing that has happened to so much modern poetry. Perfectionism is total violation, the violation of the tomb, whereas imperfection, as for instance in the gash, actually liberates the charisma. But there is no reason for either. Perfection, in the true Greek sense, avoids either excess. She offers herself in her nakedness and is there to be had. Possess her.

The trick, of course, is to know when she arrives, to recognize her when she shows up. And that is not a trick at all, you only have to know what she is. One can't rely on judgment, I mean in the sense of *estimation*. The craft has to be memorialized in the flesh, and the flesh has to be memorialized in the spirit, the life principle. Then you are free. Your work becomes what you are, and you have peace in it. Your flaws and imperfections become operative in the substance of what you do. You are delivered. She, perfection, delivers you.

Now, as concerns printing. When I finished *Triptych for the Living*, this process had not been achieved, although it was approaching. And when I swung forward into the *Psalter* it was in the hope of realization, of perfecting something. The problem of why I abandoned it is complex. Upon entering religious life I plunged into what I can only call my "monastic phase." Conversion had come in 1949 and within two years I found myself a monk in an Order. I was ambitious, spiritually ambitious. I wanted to produce a great archetypal work which would concretize something, complete something. I had always maintained that the end product of the craft of printing is the production of a masterpiece, and that, of course, requires a great text. So it was that when I perceived the opportunity of taking on the new Latin translation of the Psalms the Great Work archetype simply invaded, as the Jungians say, simply possessed me, and I threw myself into it.

Now this isn't a bad thing, actually, this possession by the archetype. Because every great work, any kind of real work, is accomplished in some loss of self, some yielding of the self to the object, to the work you're doing. You have to lose yourself to the work in order to outdo yourself, in order to do that which is greater than your own estimation decrees. This giving of the self to the work, to the subject, is crucial. To give yourself to the *subject*, in the writing of the poem, is of the essence. To give yourself to the subject, to lose yourself in the subject. Then if the craft has been memorialized in your very being you can *realize* that subject in your loss of self to it. And it is the same with printing.

So I gave myself to this effort. I lost myself, I lost myself in the great project. I swung into it and I began to print this book, which I was determined to make a perfect book. Actually, I was trying to do too much, too many things. Although it's true that I was approaching unconscious knowledge of the

140

printer's craft, I was not approaching assimilation of the monastic life. I was no more than a novice and I had no integration. If I myself were a Superior I would never let beginners undertake "masterpieces" in their novitiate, no matter how accomplished they might be. In fact I would be pretty darn sure they wouldn't launch into something stupendous until I saw signs that they had fairly matured in this new way of life. It's too much to bring off. More than once I've seen young painters come in and some Superior will give them a whole wall to paint. The kid is all fired up and the Superior is reluctant to discourage him. After all it's only a wall. If it doesn't pan out simply paint it over, and nothing lost. Actually a great deal is lost. Because once you start painting a wall a whole series of resonances are set up which utterly complicate a youth's capacity to work, you know what I mean? A wall, even in a monastery, is a public thing. The problem of community comes back on you. It's not as if you are experimenting in your studio. It becomes a collective act and all the ambiguity of your problem with your group, which in the novitiate period is severe, begins to bear down in a fantastic way.

Now all this was happening when I began printing the *Psalter*. Furthermore it became known up and down the coast that I was doing this work. First I had to appeal for money to finance my paper, and after I got started people who had seen sheets of it began to praise it. In short a whole series of pressures began to develop demanding I make good. Which, actually, is not a bad thing—part of the normal incentive of the craft. But at the same time my relation to the Order, the monastic life, was not formed enough for me to sustain this kind of pressure. I say that now. After fifteen years I have reached a point from which I could start a work like that with at least some assurance of completing it, some assurance that the monastic problem would not be riding me at the same time I was confronting the technical ones, which were monumental.

But I didn't do that. Instead I began to print, and the first year was spent perfecting the technique necessary to print folio, at the same time refining make-ready to get absolute perfection from the impression. This meant a concomitant refining of my method of damping paper, and the subsequent handling necessary to keep it damp, to keep it proper over four runnings through the press, you see. Printing quarto, four pages up, you work and turn, two times through the press, one for the black, one for the red, and that's the end of it. The original damping keeps. Printing folio, two pages up, you can't work and turn. The sheet goes through the press four times. How was I going to keep paper damp through four runs? Four slow runs on a slow handpress? And especially since I had reduced the original moistured content in order to gain crispness from the impression. Then too I was devising a new method of rolling out the ink, in order to improve on the quartos—greater evenness and uniformity, matching side for side in utter perfection going through the press. These problems had to be fought out, but I could meet them only as they arose, which meant a year of extending delays and crises, and much chagrin, much hopelessness.

Well, so. I entered the Order in 1951; I began the book that fall. I struggled till the fall of 1952 before I began to really print with consecutiveness. Through the winter of '53 and all that year I labored, but other setbacks occurred. When I started, a certain amount of manpower was available for the general monastic maintenance work, but a lot of those vocations left, and some of the jobs were reassigned to me. My time was cut down till I was really carrying a double load, getting maybe only four, five hours a day on the handpress, if that; not enough to make a complete run, and the problems were beginning to really bear down on me. Still I did get launched on it and was finally printing, and the sheets were coming out somewhere near what I wanted. I felt I had stumbled onto a magnificent format. I felt the relationship of the ink to type and type to paper was just about ideal, a terrific incentive. But it was going on too long. I had set myself a five-year period, two of which were already gone, and the problem of the monastic life was getting harder and harder to cope with. By the beginning of 1954, at a real impasse with myself, I blew up.

Now when you blow up, in order to save face, you blow from the lower position to the higher one. You don't just quit. If your psyche is acute (and whose isn't?) it finds ways of relieving itself of one project by going to a greater one, because it can't face the failure. So at this point I began to dream up the idea of becoming a priest. Not that it was entirely an unconscious ploy. I can look back on it now and see genuine charismatic elements at work there. Certainly the platform side of myself had to develop, I mean the poetry reading, lecturing, public speaking—all that had to come. And at the time I saw it as being fulfilled in the preacher, for there

142

seemed no other outlet for it in the Order. But at the same time I cannot deny that there was this tremendous impasse working against me with the book, and so I abandoned it. I just threw it up. As is well known, the sheets were taken by Mrs. Doheney, the wealthy Los Angeles collector, bound separately, and now reside as individual copies in certain libraries. They are, as you say, famous, but they are fragments.

So I went on to the priesthood. Or rather I entered the clerical novitiate and washed out in six months. And I arrived back at St. Albert's in just a frightful state of mind—a worse one than ever I faced with the *Psalter*. That taught me something, believe me. You know I had nothing. I had neither the book, nor the priesthood, nor, really, the vocation, for had I not renounced the lay brother state? I entered upon one of the worst periods of my life, which carried through till the summer of 1956, when the inner break occurred and I went down into the unconscious to find the solution to the problems that were destroying me. The Great Work archetype, which in me approaches obsession, just about finished me off. The image of the Printer and that of the Priest were both wiped out, and just in time. I began then to throw myself into the analysis of the unconscious, and went back to my poetry.

I went through a period of four or five years there, maybe more, maybe five or six years of self-analysis. As I say my poetry, which had gone dry in the clerical novitiate, was coming again. Nothing has ever wiped out the Poet in me! And it was at this period that the San Francisco Renaissance broke and I began to be called out on the platform to read my verse. Suddenly I found myself doing what I'd gone to the priesthood for—facing a living audience. I'd gone toward the priesthood in order to be a preacher, to develop the oracular dimension, the potentiality of the voice. First, remember I spoke of developing the writing, as a potentiality. Then came the development of the printing, the concretization of writing in print. Now I had to take the poem to the oral dimension. You see these steps? Each one moving toward a state of perfection in itself. So now it would be so with the voice, but I am ahead of myself. We left me midstage in printing, hung up back there around that unfinished masterwork, which I had flung off but could not escape. Why? Because I did not complete what I had begun. Of what is a magnificent fragment? All fragments are failures.

Now at last we are in a position to answer your question. In the interval after I got back to St. Albert's, before I began to go out on the platform, I tried to print. I tried two or three projects then, but none of them came off. It was as if something in me, some nerve, had broken on the *Psalter*. I had strained myself up to a decisive, perhaps fatal, psychic pitch. Perhaps the Church as muse, because she is so powerful, over-stimulated that Great Work archetype—sucked me too far out of myself, the source of my own responses. Perhaps if the text had been my own poems, something more intimate of myself, so that the work seeking completion continued the process of relating the inner and outer man, I could have finished it. As it is, I'm like a horse that's been run too hard. He has been driven beyond a point within himself, and after that can't race. Oh, he can run well enough, but he can't race, he can't *win*. So me. I can print. I've worked as a production printer for the Order, even printed *Crooked Lines* on the machine press. But to commit myself once again to a masterwork—which for me is what printing means—with the total unconscious dedication that went into the *Psalter*—I can't do it. Something chills in me when I think about it. As if, as I say, some nerve had been strained there, and, well . . . I guess that's all I can say about it.

KHERDIAN: If the Church as muse can precipitate an over-extension of self, does that not endanger the basic religious vocation? For instance, does not your ambition as a poet conflict with monastic humility? Or is this a misunderstanding on my part of the notion of humility in the Church?

ANTONINUS: There is a convention of humility, caused by the grades or the levels of the spiritual life. In the early formative phase values are conventionalized in order that they may be participated in by the incoming members, and this conventionalization of a given virtue is necessary to the whole collective enterprise. In a large corporate movement of vast scope and long tradition like monasticism, with generation after generation of men coming into it, the conventionalization of the particular virtues becomes reflexive, almost automatic. In the early phases the novice lives the conventionalization. He cannot do otherwise because he has no direct experience of what he undertakes. So you conventionalize the life, and you live it by appropriating the image that the convention sets up of the ideal, in this case humility. The function is to break a certain fixation of the ego—a certain ego-identification with the world. For in secular life the

144

worldly continuum with its own goals, its secular ambitions has done the same thing. You have the image of the successful man, and then you enter the monastery and transfer to the image of the supernaturally humble monk. He becomes your model.

Well, after a while you exhaust this conventional stage. It is the same in the world. Remember in Mark Twain's *Life on the Mississippi*, that marvelous description of the cub pilot? The novice in all these skills which have a pronounced social bearing moves forward by this artificial but necessary process. So it is with monasticism.

For in time there comes a certain crisis in the spiritual life. After the novice has become a proficient he passes through a certain dark night phase. This means that the conventionalized attitudes are no longer serviceable, and there begins an almost systematic, processive breaking down of these factors. They have now become inhibiting factors, because the end and term of the spiritual life is, really, freedom, and image-living is not freedom. What is the free man? Who but the one who has the capacity to respond to the movement and stimulus of grace, of life as it comes to him? In the beginning, as we saw, this spontaneity is inhibited by the necessity of established norms over against the unslaked ego, which has never accomplished anything. Loaded with ambition it has never participated in finality. But once it begins to possess what it desires, then it advances from proficient to expert. In the world such a one becomes an old pro. He can take ambition or lay it aside. That is to say, he does not let it impair his work. No matter what honor comes to him, no matter what fame comes to him, he performs his work. You see what I mean? He becomes the old pro.

Well, in the spiritual life it is the same. You might say the saint is, spiritually, the old pro. The young ones come in around him with all their ideals of humility, all their ideals of self-effacement, self-renouncement, self-denial; they go through their terrific efforts to achieve self-immolation. The saint, we'll say, or at least the veteran monk, if we don't want to speak of the saints. But every real monk is a saint, though few are canonized; and if he's a veteran, really up on what he's doing, he takes on a kind of sanctity. And, actually, every kind of superior dedication does that. Rexroth says somewhere of Mardersteig, the hand printer, that the craft had endowed him with a kind of sanctity, because he had entered into the freedom of his craft. It's that freedom that we intuit and know

145

to be the saintly element. The man who truly possesses his craft is saintly because he possesses freedom in it. And sanctity is freedom. The capacity to move where the need is—to respond to actual need, rather than an *a priori* formulated need. And believe me this predetermined, formulated need is a terrible thing to break, a very hard thing to break in the spiritual life.

Now, to your question. When I began to move toward that break, it was part of the same problem I was speaking of before, as a printer, in the monastic life, when I had to cease living the image because the image broke down. So now, in regard to Fame. I couldn't sustain the life any longer at the image level, yet I hadn't fought through to the unconscious resources, the opening of the inner psyche, of the Self, as Jung would say. Before I could break back into that I had to go through the Dark Night period, and at this point fame began to come to me again. I say "again" because at the moment of conversion I had worked up to Guggenheim rank as a poet, and I renounced the possibilities if offered to enter the monastery. Now, suddenly, I began to be called out into the world. The San Francisco Renaissance issue of the *Evergreen Review* travelled around the world. I was featured in *Life* and *Time* magazines. Suddenly Fame, the desire for fame or the need for fame, repressed during those long monastic years, flared up. I laid aside the presswork and took up the pen, and I laid aside the pen to mount the platform, to confront the world. I had to move out into the area of my passion, my obsession. I had to assimilate it by working through it. Of course I could have thrown up the wall again. I could have said, "No! No! Not that! I renounced all that! [laughter] Never will I again submit to the temptations and the blandishments of the world!" Well, you see, it just won't do. That's just not freedom. And since it isn't freedom, the only way you can get through to it is to eat the toad, or, better, go into the belly of the whale. You have to be like Jonah, devoured by your obsession. There comes a time when you are delivered willy-nilly into the bowels of your obsession, devoured by it, and you have to come out the other end of it—defecated or puked up, one of the two, but you've got to go through the system of the monster. For the monk, this monster has two mouths: Fame and Women. So I stand here, reeking of whale-vomit, but digested. I have gone through the gut.

KHERDIAN: You spoke of the Church as Sophia, or Holy Wisdom, and related her power to serve as muse to that. This takes on a kind of cosmological significance, doesn't it, which was given point a moment ago by your reference to yourself as a Virgoan, or perfectionist? What is your relationship to astrology?

ANTONINUS: That's difficult. It's still considered so intellectually disreputable that most thinking people refuse to take it seriously, which means the usual assumptions underlying discourse go by the board. I've come to it late. It's the most vast and complex of all the studies I've undertaken, except theology, and in some ways is the mediation between them. But I'm not very good at it. Too much arithmetic. If you can't do simple sums how can you possibly calculate transits?

I'm very glad I got through self-analysis and experienced the archetypes of the unconscious before I came to it. I doubt very much if I could have grasped the singular force of astrology unless I had done that. It's more real to approach astrology from the archetypal point of view, though anyone who is adept in astrology is certainly ready for an introduction to the unconscious. But generally the type of mind that can't grasp the concept of the archetypes, or refuses to, can't grasp the concept of astrology.

For me, astrology provides the objectivization of what is potential within me. I don't know quite how else to state that. I got into depth psychology out of personal need. Speculation for speculation's sake interests me, but I'm no good at it, no philosopher, that is. I have to fight through the battles of my life as they come up; only then do I turn and engage techniques that can help me through those battles. So with astrology. After I'd gone through the whole depth psychology bit and returned to engagement in the active life, I was ready for more objectivization. A year or so ago a friend named Terry Nichols showed me my chart, my horoscope. Suddenly many things that I'd tried to resolve in terms of depth psychology— the depth probe—became apparent to me, simply scaled out right there on the chart.

For instance, all my life I have cried out in pain when alone, or even when with someone, if I'm preoccupied. When my thought wanders from the external situation, and the attention span drops back on inner processes, then I'll hit some kind of snag, and in this momentary hang-up, this tension in myself, I'll cry out. Well, I don't like this. It is very disconcerting, not only to myself, who have never got used to it, but to others, especially others. So when I got into depth psychology I figured that it must be part of my early conditioning, and it was my hope that in dream analysis and the scrutiny of events of the pre-rational life, I could come up with some answers, some traumatic experience that I could lay bare and dispel, but no luck. Then when I was shown the chart and saw Saturn posited in the Ninth House, the House of Religion, and was told something of what that meant, I realized where the whole Dark Night of the Soul syndrome was originating, where the interior anguish was localized. I realized, for instance, that no matter what liability in my relation to my father I might pursue in order to pinpoint that particular symptom, the chart showed me that it was originating in a deeper area. Eventually I came to see that if there was a problem with the father it too was localized in the chart in the same way. The chart posits determinants that both my involuntary cry of anguish and the father-trauma turn upon together. See what I mean? The cry, the trauma, Saturn in the Ninth, these things, if not actually one and the same, are at least beads strung on the same thread. As mutually responsive symbols I suffer them out with the whole drama of reality.

Astrologically speaking, reality clicks on the principle of synchronicity. At least, that's what Jung feels. I wasn't aware of Jung's interest in astrology when I got into it. I was studying it simply because I saw something there, something relevant. But later I learned of that principle, synchronicity, and it was something my studies in mysticism enabled me to grasp quite clearly. The great simultaneity of all being from beginning to end of the temporal process and the deceptive character of time. The mystic sees the whole of reality in the unifying instant of total perception, the moment of birth and the moment of death telescoped together, the shape of the entire life posited in the single act of being. What astrology does is structure out that total act of being as it occurs for you. Your chart becomes a *mandala* upon which you meditate, widening your consciousness until all your potentialities come alive under your gaze. Call it a paradox and a mystery. But it works.

Actually, the development of modern physics has thrown the whole prospect for astrology into a more palpable light. Under the old Newtonian system a planet was nothing but a hunk of dead matter wheeling lifelessly through space, essentially inert. Modern perspectives see it as an intensively active

148

thing, not so much an object, though of course it is that, but all objects are simply localizations of energy complexes: the conversion of energy into mass. The existence of that tremendous presence out there must mean that the invisible rays or transits that compose the cosmos intersect in such a way that their potencies are activated into mass, and that this mass, being objectivized, can transmute from material to symbolic efficacy. Symbolic efficacy is the transmutation of materiality into value. For the energies to register in a meaningful way they must be translated in terms of symbolic force.

A couple of weeks ago I wrote the first poem I've written all year. I'd seen the film *Dr. Zhivago* the night before in San Francisco—not a good film, either, unfortunately. But the way Zhivago lost Lara, the loss of her, turning the corner out of his life—that haunted me. Too much of myself in it not to be moved by it. And the next day I sat down and this poem began to come, the closing of a love. And naturally I took it as something to do with the movie, because that had been on my mind. What could be more obvious?

Well, a week later I happened to look at the Ephemeris for the month and noticed that the planet Venus moved onto the 29th degree of Capricorn the day I wrote the poem. Now it so happens that Capricorn 29 is the degree Uranus held when I was born. Suddenly I realized about the poem. The Sabian symbol is feminine: a gypsy woman reading tea leaves, "the mind has its ultimate focus in eternal and universal coordinates, and ever tends to fit the exigencies of practical living into some pattern of possible consummations." Now Uranus is the planet of inspiration, and is in my Fifth House, the House of Creativity. Anything that touches that degree is going to stimulate the Uranian response. Not only so, but a few days before that, Venus had entered the Virgoan Fifth House, once again the House of Creativity, the House of Love, of Pleasure. The fact that Venus was not only in the house, but went straight across Capricorn 29—well, this poem emerged. Let me read it for you.

Gold gropes the dawn. Time wavers on the interdicted face.
A sovereignty of distance shapes and fashions
The contours of those long abandoned passions.
Charred fragments of desire flake upward from that place.

Outside, the visionary rainfalls veil the day.
The mystic semblance of an ancient sorrow
Trembles the nighttime of our vast tomorrow.
Reluctant as the light they fade and glide away.

149

Her face reenters time. God of all tangled deeps
    Revokes the sureties of old reliance,
    Darker than the stonefalls of defiance.
She murmurs in her dream, and stirs herself, and sleeps.

Well, what does it mean, astrologically speaking? To me it means that the poem and the planet and the residual potentiality inhering in the degree from the presence of Uranus there at birth achieved, in some metaphysical dimension, approximation. What I said earlier about symbolic force, the efficacy of symbolic force. Anyone who knows the archetypes knows that symbols have force, awesome force. The archetypes of my unconscious were touched at that moment, and the deep, most profound roots of my experience were stirred. Venus, the love, Uranus, the inspiration or quickening, these two archetypes momentarily conjoined, like a musical chord. Some finality was placed on an old pain, something was healed. I was delivered. The sensitivity of Saturn is in there too, because in my chart the three of them make the Grand Trine. That sensitivity of loss, Saturn, touching the spirit of Love in the creative throes of inspiration. No sense in overstressing it, however. None of this is necessary to an understanding of the poem—that can go on at an entirely different dimension. But as an artist I have learned when the archetypes are in play. And from studying astrology, I have learned something of what sets them in play.

For when I look back over the chart and see a thing like that, it confirms the mystery, rather than dispels it, in my own mind. I am at one with the wholeness of things. I don't feel like a mechanical agent, as if something out there triggered something in here. I feel more as if the cycle of the cosmos had moved around in a certain way, and out of that movement I, too, was moved. I responded, the poem was my response. And the poem is increased in its dimension in my mind, for having emerged out of such a context, then if I were to localize it back at simply the more personalistic level—that I had happened to write because I happened to see a film the night before. Well, I did. The personalistic element is here also; but the larger dimension, the greater form to me is the fact that the sum of things was centering upon that particular point in time. Nothing is lost, but a great deal is gained. For a very short interval, Venus swims into my Fifth House, crosses Capricorn 29, and is gone. Like Lara! Just turns the corner and enters another dimension, something I can't see yet, may never possess. It's very meaningful. And many old pains, many old scars, are transmuted into accent marks that glow with a life they never had before. What was once my pain becomes not only bearable, I had already gained that. Now it became beautiful. What more can one ask?

+ triptych for the living
poems by william everson, with prints
by mary fabilli. the seraphim press: 1951

TITLE PAGE, NO. 12

BOOKS AND BROADSIDES

1. THESE ARE THE RAVENS, by Bill Everson. San Leandro, Calif., Greater West Publishing Co. (Pamphlet Series of Western Poets), 1935.

   Printed wrappers. 1000 copies only.

2. SAN JOAQUIN, by William Everson. Los Angeles, Calif., The Ward Ritchie Press, June, 1939.

   Brown decorative paper boards, cloth backed spine. Title page dec oration by Hubert Buel repeated on front cover. 100 copies only.

3. THE MASCULINE DEAD: Poems, 1938-1940, by William Everson. Prairie City, Illinois, The Press of James A. Decker, 1942.

   Fabricoid over boards. About 200 copies only. The 100 copies received by the author as royalty payment contain the publisher's errata slip which the author tipped-on to face p. 44. All of the copies received by the author were bound in green fabricoid, with lettering same as above, and without the errata slip, which would indicate that all copies placed for sale by the publisher were issued without an errata slip. The one such copy inspected was bound in maroon fabricoid.

4. X WAR ELEGIES, by William Everson. Waldport, Oregon (Camp Angel), Untide Press, 1943.

   Blue printed wrappers lettered in black and yellow. The second state wrapper lettering is in black and red, of which far fewer copies were printed. Illustrations and typography by Kemper Nomland, Jr. About 1000 mimeographed copies only. This was the first publication of the Untide Press.

5. THE WALDPORT POEMS, by William Everson. Waldport, Oregon, Untide Press, July, 1944.

   Decorative wrappers. Designed and with linoleum blocks by Clayton James. 975 copies only.

6. WAR ELEGIES, by William Everson. Waldport, Oregon, Untide Press, November, 1944.

   Decorative wrappers. First letterpress edition. Designed and with linoleum blocks and line cuts by Kemper Nowland, Jr. 975 copies only. This edition, which consists of eleven poems, contains, in addition, *War Elegy V*, which is included here in its proper chronological location.

7. THE RESIDUAL YEARS: Poems, 1940-1941, by William Everson. Waldport, Oregon, The Untide Press, December, 1944.

Gray decorative wrappers. Designed by Wm. Eshelman and illustrated by the author. 330 mimeographed copies only.

8. POEMS: MCMXLII, by William Everson. Waldport, Oregon, Untide Press, 1944-1945.

Decorative wrappers. Cover and erratum decorations by Clayton James. The only Untide Press item printed solely by William Everson. 500 copies only.

9. THE EQUINOX PRESS, by William Everson. Berkeley, Calif., Autumn, 1947.

Broadside. "Announcing the establishment of a private press." Written, designed, hand-set, and printed on the handpress by William Everson, with a block print by Mary Fabilli. 500 copies only.

10. THE RESIDUAL YEARS, by William Everson. New York, N.Y., A New Directions Book, 1948.

Decorative paper boards, cloth backed spine. Issued with a dust jacket, the inside front flap containing an unacknowledged blurb by Kenneth Rexroth. 1000 copies only. This is essentially a cumulative edition of the previous publications. It consists of three parts, in reverse chronology: the first part reprints *The Waldport Poems*, and adds to it four more sections, inclusively, called Chronicle of Division. The second part is a complete reprinting of *X War Elegies*, *War Elegies*, *The Residual Years* [1944], and *Poems: MCMXLII*. The third part is a selection by Kenneth Rexroth from *These Are the Ravens*, *San Joaquin*, and *The Masculine Dead*.

11. A PRIVACY OF SPEECH; Ten Poems in Sequence, by William Everson. Berkeley, Calif., The Equinox Press, 1949.

Gray decorative paper over boards, with vellum backed spine. Lettering on spine stamped in gold. Block print decorations by Mary Fabilli. 100 copies only. Designed, hand-set, printed on the handpress and bound by William Everson.

12. TRIPTYCH FOR THE LIVING, by William Everson. Oakland, Calif., The Seraphim Press, 1951.

Goat vellum, with orange ties. Prints by Mary Fabilli. Printed on the handpress and bound by William Everson, at Maurin House, a Catholic Worker house of hospitality in Oakland, California. 200 copies, of which less than 100 were issued, the remaining sheets destroyed.

13a. AT THE EDGE [by Brother Antoninus]. n.p. [Oakland, Calif.] [Albertus Magnus Press], n.d. [1958].

Broadside. 100 copies were printed by the author in 1952.

13b. In 1958 about 80 copies remained and these were offered for sale by the publisher in a narrow black wooden frame with each copy signed by the poet/printer.

14. An Age Insurgent, by Brother Antoninus. San Francisco, Calif., Blackfriars Publications of the West. n.d. [May, 1959].

Black wrappers. Number of copies unknown. Probably less than 100 copies were issued; the remaining copies are believed to have been destroyed.

15a. The Crooked Lines of God; Poems 1949-1954, by Brother Antoninus. n.p. [Detroit, Michigan], The University of Detroit Press (Number One of the Contemporary Poets Series), October, 1959.

Gray paper boards, with black cloth spine, gold lettered. Issued with a dust jacket. Printed by the author in Oakland, California. The first edition is so designated on the colophon page. 1000 copies.

15b. Reissued April, 1960, in an edition of 1000 copies, also printed by the author at the same site. The second edition may be identified by the following points:
1. The copyright page carries the designation Second Edition.
2. The colophon device is red.
3. The colophon date is April, 1960.

Changes & Additions: *triptych* for *the uncouth, the coming,* and *the wise,* marginal subtitle, pp. 13-18; *cross-making* for *the cross-making,* marginal subtitle, pp. 21-22; "Be not as the horse and mule, that have no understanding", top of p. 42; *massacre* for *the massacre,* marginal subtitle, pp. 51-53; *annulment* for *the annulment,* marginal subtitle, pp. 86-87; *phoenix* for *the phoenix,* marginal subtitle, p. 88.

15c. Reissued 1962 in two bindings of 500 copies each:
1. Black cloth over boards. Stamping on spine identical with the first two editions.
2. Wrappers; the dust jacket for the cloth issue has been made to serve as the wrapper cover.

15d. A second impression for the third edition was issued in the fall of 1964 in a printing of 500 copies, all clothbound in the same binding as the third edition. The entire third edition was printed in Detroit by photo lithography, with the spinal lettering being made from the first edition cut. All changes and additions from the second edition were incorporated.

Errata: *That fragile* for *That strengthless.* p. 20, line 18; *Assisi* for *Asissi,* p. 57; *His* for *his,* p. 59, line 14; *When the horse, his knees failed of driving, lay down and died in the earth,* inserted, p. 49, line 20;—*Psalm XXXI,* beneath epigraph, p. 42.

16. There Will Be Harvest, by William Everson. Berkeley, Calif., University of California General Library, September, 1960.

French fold. Decorative design on title repeated in text. Printed by Kenneth J. Carpenter in an edition of 200 copies. Woodcut by K.J.C.

17. THE YEAR'S DECLENSION, by William Everson. Berkeley, Calif., University of California at Berkeley, 1961.

Gray decorative paper over boards. Printed by Kenneth John Carpenter on the Berkeley Albion in the rare books department of the general library of the University of California at Berkeley. Initials and signs cut in wood are by K.J.C. 100 copies, of which 50 copies were offered for sale. All copies signed by the author beneath the colophon.

18a. THE HAZARDS OF HOLINESS; Poems 1957-1960, by Brother Antoninus. Garden City, New York, Doubleday & Company, Inc., June, 1962.

Red cloth over boards in the dust jacket. The copyright page contains the designation First Edition. There were 2000 copies printed for the first edition.

18b. Second printing. 1000 copies.

18c. Third printing. 2000 copies. There were no binding, textual, or dust jacket changes for these reprintings.

19a. THE POET IS DEAD (a Memorial for Robinson Jeffers), by Brother Antoninus. San Francisco, Calif., The Auerhahn Press, March, 1964.

White paper over boards with violet leather spine. Title label on spine lettered in gold. Issued with a plain white dust jacket. 205 copies, of which

19b. 5 copies, not for sale, in white monks cloth slip case. All copies signed by the author on leaf facing last page of text.

20a. THE ROSE OF SOLITUDE, by Brother Antoninus. n.p. [Berkeley, Calif.], Oyez, 1964.

Broadside. 350 copies only. Printed by the Auerhahn Press for Oyez. No. 2 in the publisher's series of 10 broadsides.

20b. 27 copies of each broadside in the series were later signed by the poets and laid in a heavy linen board folder for separate sale. Only 25 of these sets, which were prepared in 1965, were offered for sale.

21a. THE BLOWING OF THE SEED, by William Everson. New Haven, Conn., Henry W. Wenning, 1966.

Decorative paper over boards, leather backed spine, with lettering blind stamped. 218 copies signed by the poet. Of this number the first

21b. 3 copies are lettered a, b, & c, and are respectively for poet, publisher, and printer.

21c. Copies i to xv are for friends of the poet and publisher. Copies not lettered are numbered in sequence. This sequence of poems was written in 1946 and belongs to the period of *The Residual Years*. This is their first printing.

22a. SINGLE SOURCE: The Early Poems of William Everson [1934-1940]. Berkeley, Calif., Oyez, April, 1966.

Decorative paper over boards, linen backed spine, gold stamped. Issued with a dust jacket. An undeterminate number of copies in the first issue spell language *langauge*, page ix, lines 16-17. Designed and printed by Graham Mackintosh. 1000 copies only, of which

22b. 25 are numbered and signed by the poet and have been individually bound by Dorothy Hawley in a beveled spine, cloth backed, which is otherwise identical with the trade edition.

FUGITIVE PIECES & EPHEMERA

23. FOURTEEN / POEMS / 1940-1941 / BY / WILLIAM EVERSON / Selma, California/*The Broken Acres Press*/1943.

Title page proof sheet for an unpublished book. The type was set by James Atkisson and William Everson in Sanger, California, in 1942. Also extant are p. 9, which contains the poem "IV," which was retitled, "War Elegy II" and collected in the *War Elegies* books, and also as, "Now in These Days," in *The Residual Years* [1948]; pp. 12-13, which contain the poem "V," which was retitled "War Elegy III" and collected in the *War Elegies* books, and also as "One Born of This Time" in *The Residual Years* [1948]; p. 14, which contains the poem "VI," which was retitled "War Elegy IV" and collected in the *War Elegies* books.

24. THE FINE ARTS AT WALDPORT. Waldport, Oregon, Committee on Fine Arts, C. P. S. Camp 56, The Untide Press, n.d. [1943].

Tan wrappers. [8] pp. mimeographed announcement laid in. Text by William Everson, who was then chairman of the Committee on Fine Arts.

25. VOCATION-COMMUNITY. Elgin, Illinois, Brethren CPS, August, 1945.

[6] pp. mimeographed brochure. Page [3] contains "Vocational Art and Community Living," by William Everson.

26. ALLELUIA/DEO GRATIAS. n.p. [Berkeley, Calif.], The Equinox Press, Christmas, 1948.

White folder. Block print of an angel in green on the front cover by Mary Fabilli. Printed on the inside back cover in black is a quotation in Latin and English from John 1:14. The title is printed above and below the text and is in red as is the colophon, which is printed on the back cover. 85 copies were printed on the handpress and were sent as season's greetings by William and Mary Everson.

27. AT THE EDGE: a poem/by Brother Antoninus, O.P., Oakland, Calif., The Albertus Magnus Press, n.d. [1958].

Broadsheet. Advertisement mailer written by Brother Antoninus announcing the sale of the broadside, *At the Edge*.

28. A Fragment for the Birth of God, by Brother Antoninus, O.P., Oakland, Calif., The Albertus Magnus Press, St. Albert's College, May, 1958.

White folder. Title on front cover, as above, with the additional word, *Deus*, as a decorative element. The poem has been printed on a separate sheet which has been cut to uniform size and laid in. Libra type, printed in two colors: black and terra-cotta. Written, designed and printed by Brother Antoninus. Offered for sale at twenty-five cents. 1000 copies, of which between 800-900 were destroyed by a novice lay brother at St. Albert's in 1959.

29. A Fragment for the Birth of God. Oakland, Calif., St. Albert's College, n.d. [Christmas, 1959].

French fold. The title in terra-cotta, and a wood-block print by the author in blue, appear on the front cover. Lettering on inside top is blue; the poem on the inside bottom half is in terra-cotta. Issued with an envelope made from the same cream-colored paper stock. Written, designed, and printed by Brother Antoninus in an edition of 6000 copies as the house Christmas card.

30. A Fragment for the Birth of God. n.p. [Oakland, Calif.], [St. Albert's College], n.d. [1963?]

Folder. The title in terra-cotta, and a woodblock print by the author in blue, appear on the front cover. The poem is printed in terra-cotta on the inside back cover.

31. The Catholic and Creativity: Louis Merton, O.C.S.O., William Davidson, M.D., Brother Antoninus, O.P., Collegeville, Minnesota, The American Benedictine Review [September-December, 1960].

Wrappers. Extract from The American Benedictine Review.

PERIODICAL AND NEWSPAPER CONTRIBUTIONS

[*All contributions are poems unless otherwise noted. This section is divided into two parts. This first part contains contributions by William Everson.*]

32. The Caravan, Vol. V, No. 1. Fresno, Calif., Fresno State College, December, 1931.

Edited by Glenna Walters. Contains "Gypsy Dance." Uncollected.

33. The Caravan, Vol. 8, No. 1. Fresno, Calif., Fresno State College, November, 1934.

Edited by Anne Spalding. Contains "Autumn Song," "Compensations," and "Deserted Garden." All uncollected.

34. The Caravan, Vol. 8, No. 2. Fresno, Calif., Fresno State College, April, 1935.

Edited by Anne Spalding. Contains "First Winter Storm," "October Tragedy," "Poem," and "Winter Plowing." "Poem" was collected as the title poem in *These Are the Ravens*, where all of these poems were collected. "Winter Plowing" and "First Winter Storm" were also collected in *The Residual Years* [1948].

158

35. Westward. San Leandro, Calif., Greater West Publishing Co., August, 1935.

Edited by Hans A. Hoffman. Contains "These Are the Ravens," and "Do Not Brood for Long." Both poems were collected in *These Are the Ravens*.

36. Carmel Pine Cone, Vol. XXI, No. 38, Carmel, Calif., September 20, 1935.

Contains "Tor House." Collected in *These Are the Ravens*.

37. Westward, Vol. IV, No. 10. San Leandro, Calif., Greater West Publishing Co., October, 1935.

Edited by Hans A. Hoffman. Contains "Winter Plowing." Collected in *These Are the Ravens* and *The Residual Years* [1948].

38. The Pine Cone, Vol. XXII, No. 8. Carmel, Calif., February 21, 1936.

Contains "Here the Rock Sleeps." Uncollected.

39. The Caravan, Vol. 9, No. 1. Fresno, Calif., Fresno State College, April, 1936.

Edited by Eunice Lowe. Contains "The Flesh and the Bone." Collected in *San Joaquin* as "Fish-Eaters."

40. Literary America, Vol. III, No. 6. New York, N.Y., June, 1936.

Contains "The Flesh and the Bone." See above.

41. The Pine Cone, Vol. XXIII, No. 2. Carmel, Calif., January 8, 1937.

Contains "The Eye Sees but the Heart." Collected as "Fog" in *San Joaquin* and *The Residual Years* [1948].

42. Poetry: A Magazine of Verse, Vol. L, No. 3. Chicago, Ill., Poetry, June, 1937.

Edited by Morton Dauwen Zabel. Contains "We in the Fields," and "Dust and the Glory." Both collected in *San Joaquin*, the last poem as "Attila."

43. The Saturday Review of Literature, Vol. XVI, No. 16. New York, N.Y., The Saturday Review Company, Inc., August 14, 1937.

Contains "Sleep." Collected in *San Joaquin*.

44. The Pine Cone, Vol. XXIII, No. 34. Carmel, Calif., August 20, 1937.

Contains "Who Worships the Sun." Collected as "August" in *San Joaquin*, and in *The Residual Years* [1948].

159

45. The Phoenix, Vol. I, No. 3. Woodstock, New York, Autumn, 1938.

Contains "Poem." Revised and collected in *The Masculine Dead*, and *The Residual Years* [1948] as "Orion."

46. Caravan, Vol. XIII, No. 1. Fresno, Calif., Associated Student Body of Fresno State College, November, 1939.

Edited by Thomas Carlile. Contains "We Walk the Young Earth: Conejo, California." Uncollected.

47. Caravan, Vol. XIII, No. 2. Fresno, Calif., Associated Student Body of Fresno State College, January, 1940.

Edited by Thomas Carlile. Contains "The Ruin." Collected in *The Masculine Dead and The Residual Years* [1948].

48. Poetry: A Magazine of Verse, Vol. LV, No. V. Chicago, Ill., Poetry, February, 1940.

Edited by George Dillon. Contains "The Sign," by William Herber (pseudonym). Uncollected.

49. Poetry: A Magazine of Verse, Vol. LVI, No. 11. Chicago, Ill., Poetry, May, 1940.

Edited by George Dillon. Pages 108-9 contain a letter *To the Editor* by William Everson.

50. Experimental Review, No. 2. Woodstock, New York, November, 1940.

Edited by Robert Duncan and Sanders Russell. Contains "Feast Day." Collected in *The Masculine Dead* and in *The Residual Years* [1948].

51. The Untide, Vol. I, No. 5. Waldport, Oregon, The Untide, February 6, 1943.

Edited by C. R. Bunyan. Contains "Trifles." Reprinted from *San Joaquin*.

52. The Tide, Vol. II, No. 2. n.p. [Waldport, Oregon], The Tide, February, 1943.

Edited by C. R. Bunyan. Contains "Clouds." Reprinted from *San Joaquin*.

53. The Untide, Vol. I, No. 6, Waldport, Oregon, The Untide, February 13, 1943.

Contains "War Elegy I (The Registration, October 16, 1940)." Collected in both *War Elegies* books and in *The Residual Years* [1948] as "The Vow."

54. The Untide, Vol. I, No. 7. Waldport, Oregon, The Untide, February 20, 1943.

Contains "War Elegy II (The Lottery, October 29, 1941)." Collected in both *War Elegies* books and in *The Residual Years* [1948] as "Now in These Days."

55. The Untide, Vol. I, No. 8. Waldport, Oregon, The Untide, February 28, 1943.

Contains "War Elegy III." Collected in both *War Elegies* books and in *The Residual Years* [1948] as "One Born of This Time."

56. The Untide, Vol. I, No. 9. Waldport, Oregon, The Untide, March 5, 1943.

Contains "War Elegy IV (The Prime Minister's Address, February, 1941)." Collected in both *War Elegies* books and in *The Residual Years* [1948] as "The Unkillable Knowledge."

57. The Untide, Vol. I, No. 10. Waldport, Oregon, March 13, 1943.

Contains "War Elegy V," and "War Elegy VI." Collected in both *War Elegies* books and in *The Residual Years* [1948] as "A Winter Ascent," and "Eastward the Armies."

58. The Untide, Vol. I, No. 11. Waldport, Oregon, The Untide, March 20, 1943.

Contains "War Elegy VII." Collected in both *War Elegies* books and in *The Residual Years* [1948] as "The Raid."

59. The Untide, Vol. I, No. 12. Waldport, Oregon, The Untide, n.d. [1943].

Contains "War Elegy X (The Internment, Waldport, Oregon, January, 1943)." Collected in both *War Elegies* books and in *The Residual Years* [1948] as poem "XI" in part one of "Chronicle of Division."

60. The Tide, Vol. II, No. 3. Waldport, Oregon, The Tide, March, 1943.

Edited by Everett Groff. Contains "The Rancho." Collected in *The Residual Years* [1944] as "As long as we looked lay the Low Low Country" [first line], and in the 1948 edition as "The Residual Years."

61. The Tide, Vol. II, No. 4. Waldport, Oregon. The Tide, n.d. [April, 1943].

Edited by Don Kimmel. Contains "Approach to the City." Collected in *The Residual Years* [1944] as "Breaking Back from the Sea," and in the 1948 edition as "The Approach."

62. The Illiterati, Vol. I, No. 1. Wyeth, Oregon, The Illiterati, Spring, 1943.

Edited by Kermit Sheets and Kemper Nomland, Jr. Contains 2 *War Elegies:* "(The Registration, October 16, 1940)" [War Elegy III], and "(The Lottery, October 29, 1941)" [War Elegy IV]. Collected in both *War Elegies* books and in *The Residual Years* [1948].

63. The Illiterati. n.p. [Wyeth, Oregon], The Illiterati, Summer, 1943.

Edited by Kermit Sheets and Kemper Nomland, Jr. Contains "Do You Not Doubt?" Collected in both of *The Residual Years.*

64. The Tide, Vol. II, No. 5. Waldport, Oregon, The Tide, July, 1943.

Edited by Don Kimmel. Contains "War Elegy X (The Internment, Waldport, Oregon, January, 1943)." Collected in *The Residual Years* [1948].

65. The Compass, Vol. I, No. 6, West Compton, New Hampshire, Spring, 1944.

Edited by Martin Pounch. Contains "No, Not Ever, in No Time." Collected in both of *The Residual Years;* in the 1948 edition as "The Impossible Choices."

66. The Illiterati, No. 3. Wyeth, Oregon, The Illiterati, Summer, 1944.

Edited by Kermit Sheets and Kemper Nomland, Jr. Contains "Thou Lying with Woman." Collected in both of *The Residual Years.*

67. The Compass, Vol. II, Nos. 1 & 2, Waldport, Oregon, Summer-Fall, 1944.

Edited by Martin Pounch. Contains "I Call to Mind That Violent Man." Collected in *The Residual Years* [1948] as "The Outlaw."

68. The Illiterati, No. 4. Waldport, Oregon, The Illiterati, Summer, 1945.

Edited by Kermit Sheets and Kemper Nomland, Jr. Contains "The Revolutionist." Collected in *Poems: MCMXLII*, and in *The Residual Years* [1948].

69. The Compass, Vol. II, Nos. 3 & 4. Waldport, Oregon, Compass, n.d. [1945].

Edited by Martin Pounch. Contains "Yet Must the Man Marvel." Collected in *The Residual Years* [1948] as poem "VI" in part II of "Chronicle of Division."

70. Circle, No. 9. Berkeley, Calif., Circle, 1946.

Edited by George Leite. Contains "The Release." Collected in *The Residual Years* [1948] as poem "VI" of part IV of "Chronicle of Division."

71. The Ark, Vol. I, No. 1. San Francisco, Calif., Spring, 1947.

Contains "If I Hide My Hand." Uncollected.

72. California Library Bulletin, Vol. IX, No. 4. Los Angeles, Calif., California Library Association, June, 1948.

Edited by Neal Harlow. Contains "The Ruin," from *The Masculine Dead*, and "San Joaquin" and "Walls," from *San Joaquin.*

73. The Illiterati, No. 5. Pasadena, Calif., The Illiterati, 1948.

Edited by William Eshelman, Tom Polk Miller, and Kemper Nomland, Jr. Contains "The Flesh Waits On." Collected as "Poem IX" in *A Privacy of Speech*.

74. Berkeley: A Journal of Modern Culture, No. 7. Berkeley, Calif., 1949.

Edited by James Schevill. Contains "The Dusk," and "The First Absence." Both poems were collected in *The Year's Declension*, the last poem as "The First Absence: I."

75. Berkeley: A Journal of Modern Culture, No. 8. Berkeley, Calif., 1949.

Edited by James Schevill. Contains "The Dance." Collected in *The Year's Declension*.

76. The Pacific Spectator; a Journal of Interpretation, Vol. III, No. 4. Stanford, Calif., Autumn, 1949.

Contains "Time of Year: Three Poems of Autumn." Uncollected.

77. Occident. n.p. [Berkeley, Calif.], Associated Students of the University of California, Fall, 1949.

Edited by Kenneth Pettitt. Contains an article written for "The Poet and Poetry—a Symposium." Uncollected.

78. The Tiger's Eye, No. 9. New York, N.Y., October, 1949.

Edited by Ruth Stephen. Contains "The Carrousel." Uncollected.

79. The Catholic Worker, Vol. XVI, No. 7. New York, N.Y., December, 1949.

Edited by Dorothy Day. Contains "Triptych for the Living," consisting of: "The Uncouth, The Coming, and The Wise." Collected in *Triptych for the Living, An Age Insurgent*, and *The Crooked Lines of God*, and anthologized in *New Directions 12*.

80. The Catholic Worker, Vol. XVI, No. 9. New York, N.Y., February, 1950.

Edited by Dorothy Day. Contains "In the Dream's Recess." Collected in *An Age Insurgent* and *The Year's Declension*.

81. The Book Club of California Quarterly News Letter, Vol. XV, No. 2. n.p. [San Francisco, Calif.], Spring, 1950.

Contains the article, "Latter-Day Handpress." Collected in *Second Reading; Selections from the Quarterly News Letter 1933-1963*.

82. The Catholic Worker, Vol. XVII. New York, N.Y., September, 1950.

Edited by Dorothy Day. Contains "Making of the Cross." Collected in *Triptych for the Living, An Age Insurgent*, and *The Crooked Lines of God*, and anthologized in *The Tree and the Master*.

163

83. The Catholic Worker, Vol. XVII. New York, N.Y., November, 1950.

Edited by Dorothy Day. Contains "At the Edge." Published as a broadside in 1958.

84. The Catholic Worker, Vol. XVII, New York, N.Y., February, 1951.

Edited by Dorothy Day. Contains "Flight in the Desert." Collected in *Triptych for the Living*, *An Age Insurgent*, and *The Crooked Lines of God*.

85. The Catholic Worker, Vol. XVII. New York, N.Y., May, 1951.

Edited by Dorothy Day. Contains "Maurin House, Oakland." Collected as "Hospice of the Word, Part I" in *The Crooked Lines of God*.

86. The Catholic Worker, Vol. XVIII, No. 3. New York, N.Y., October, 1951.

Edited by Dorothy Day. Contains "Maurin House, Oakland: Part II." Collected as "Hospice of the Word, Part II" in *The Crooked Lines of God*.

87. The Catholic Worker, Vol. XVIII, No. 6. New York, N.Y., The Catholic Worker, January, 1952.

Edited by Dorothy Day. Contains "The Burning Book." Uncollected.

88. The Catholic Worker, Vol. XVIII, No. 12. New York, N.Y., The Catholic Worker, July-August, 1952.

Edited by Dorothy Day. Contains "Full Summer." Collected as "Past Solstice" in *An Age Insurgent*.

[*The contributions to follow, with one exception, are by Brother Antoninus.*]

89. The Catholic Worker, Vol. XVIII, No. 15. New York, N.Y., The Catholic Worker, November, 1952.

Edited by Dorothy Day. Contains "A Canticle to the Waterbirds." Collected in *An Age Insurgent* and *The Crooked Lines of God*, and anthologized in *The New American Poetry: 1945-1960* .

90. The Catholic Worker, Vol. XVIII, No. 17. New York, N.Y., The Catholic Worker, January, 1953.

Edited by Dorothy Day. Contains "The Massacre of the Holy Innocents." Collected in *The Crooked Lines of God*.

91. The Catholic Worker, Vol. XX, No. 1. New York, N.Y., The Catholic Worker, July-August, 1953.

Edited by Dorothy Day. Contains "A Jubilee." Collected as "A Jubilee for Peter Martyr" in *The Crooked Lines of God.*

92. Voices, No. 153. Vinalhaven, Maine, January-April, 1954.

Edited by Harold Vinal. Contains "Under a Keeping Spring." Collected in *The Year's Declension*, and anthologized in *Borestone Mountain Poetry Awards 1955*.

93. The Book Club of California Quarterly News Letter, Vol. XIX, No. 3. n.p. [San Francisco, Calif.], Summer, 1954.

Contains the article, "Printer as Contemplative." Uncollected.

94. Evergreen Review, Vol. I, No. 2. New York, N.Y., Grove Press, Inc., 1957.

Edited by Barney Rosset and Donald Allen. Contains "The South Coast," "A Penitential Psalm," "Annul in Me My Manhood," and "Out of the Ash." Also contained is a photograph of Brother Antoninus by Harry Redl. All of the poems were collected in *The Crooked Lines of God*. "The South Coast" was anthologized in *The New American Poetry: 1945-1960*.

95. The Monitor. San Francisco, Calif., Archdiocese of San Francisco, November 1, 1957.

Contains "Francis Thompson: One Great Taste of the Sky," a book review by Brother Antoninus of Francis J. Connelly's, *A Man Has Wings*.

96. The Chicago Review, Vol. XII, No. 3. Chicago, Ill., The University of Chicago, Autumn, 1958.

Edited by Paul Carroll. Contains "A Siege of Silence." Collected in *The Hazards of Holiness*.

97. The Texas Quarterly, Vol. I, No. 4. Austin, Texas. The University of Texas, Winter, 1958.

Contains "A Canticle to the Christ in the Holy Eucharist." Collected in *The Crooked Lines of God* and anthologized in *Today's Poets*.

98. Fresco: The University of Detroit Quarterly, Vol. IX, No. 2. Detroit, Michigan, Winter, 1958.

Edited by Steve Eisner. Contains "The Encounter." Collected in *An Age Insurgent* and *The Crooked Lines of God*.

99. The Monitor. San Francisco, Calif., December 5, 1958.

Contains a book review by Brother Antoninus of *The Word Is Love*, by Sister Maura, S.S.N.D.

100. Four Quarters, Vol. VIII, No. 2. Philadelphia, Pa., La Salle College, January, 1959.

Contains "The Quittance of the Wound." Collected in *An Age Insurgent*.

101. Fresco: The University of Detroit Quarterly, Vol. IX, No. 3. Detroit, Michigan, 1959.

Edited by Steve Eisner. Contains a biographical sketch and a bibliography of Brother Antoninus' books written by himself, and his poem "A Savagery of Love," which was collected in *The Crooked Lines of God*.

102. The Owl, Vol. XLVI, No. 3. Santa Clara, Calif., University of Santa Clara, Spring, 1959.

Contains "Rainy Easter." Collected in *The Year's Declension*.

103. Big Table, Vol. I, No. 2. Chicago, Ill., Big Table, Inc., Summer, 1959.

Edited by Paul Carroll. Contains "Zone of Death." Collected in *The Hazards of Holiness*.

104. Fresco: The University of Detroit Quarterly, Vol. IX, No. 4. Detroit, Michigan, Summer, 1959.

Edited by Steve Eisner. Contains the article, "Dionysius and the Beat Generation." Uncollected.

105. Jubilee; a Magazine of the Church and Her People, Vol. VIII, No. 4. New York, N.Y., A.M.D.G. Publishing Co., August, 1959.

Edited by Edward Rice. Contains "Jacob and the Angel." Collected in *The Hazards of Holiness*. Anthologized in *Modern Religious Poems*.

106. America. New York, N.Y., January 16, 1960.

Page 435 contains "Disclaimer," a letter to the editor from Brother Antoninus.

107. The Fresco Sampler: The University of Detroit Quarterly, Vol. X, No. 3. Detroit, Michigan, Summer, 1960.

Edited by Steve Eisner. Contains "The Encounter." Collected in *An Age Insurgent* and *The Crooked Lines of God*.

108. The American Benedictine Review, Vol. XI, Nos. 3 & 4. Collegeville, Minn., St. John's University, September-December, 1960.

Contains from a symposium, "The Artist and the Religious Life," which is a transcription from a tape recorded interview that was heavily footnoted for publication in this magazine.

109. Jubilee; a Magazine of the Church and Her People, Vol. VIII, No. 8. New York, N.Y., A.M.D.G. Publishing Co., December, 1960.

Edited by Ed. Rice. Contains "A Canticle to the Great Mother of God." Collected in *The Hazards of Holiness*.

110. Four Quarters, Vol. X, No. 2. Philadelphia, Pa., La Salle College, January, 1961.

Contains Brother Antoninus' contribution to a symposium on the teaching of creative writing.

111. Damascus Road, Vol. I, No. 1. Allentown, Pennsylvania, Damascus Road, 1961.

Edited by Charles Shahoud Hanna. Contains "The Word." Collected in *The Hazards of Holiness*.

112. Sewanee Review, Vol. LXIX, No. 2. Sewanee, Tenn., University of the South, Spring, 1961.

Edited by Monroe K. Spears. Contains a letter from Brother Antoninus to the editor discussing James Dickey's review of *The Crooked Lines of God*. Dickey's reply is included.

113. Sewanee Review, Vol. LXIX, No. 3. Sewanee, Tenn., University of the South, Summer, 1961.

Edited by Monroe K. Spears. Contains a letter to James Dickey and Dickey's rejoinder.

114. Revista de la Universidad de Mexico, Vol. XV, No. 11. Mexico City, Mexico, The University of Mexico, July, 1961.

Contains "Salmo Penitenical" (Penitential Psalm, from *The Crooked Lines of God*), and "Cántico a Las Aves Acuáticas" (A Canticle to the Waterbirds, from *An Age Insurgent* and *The Crooked Lines of God*). Translation by Cardinal Ernesto.

115. Inscape, Vol. I, No. 3. Ellensburg, Washington, Central Washington State College, Fall, 1961.

Contains a transcription from a reading; the poems have been omitted and the commentary only has been printed here as "The Poet."

116. El Pez y La Serpiente (Esta Revista Se Publica Auspiciada por Casa Pellas), No. 3. Managua, Nicaragua, March, 1962.

Contains "Salmo Penitencial" (Penitential Psalm), and "Cántico a Las Aves Acuáticas" (A Canticle to the Waterbirds). Translation from *Revista de la Universidad de Mexico*.

117. Poetry Northwest, Vol. III, No. 1. Seattle, Washington, University of Washington, Spring, 1962.

Edited by Carolyn Kizer, Nelson Bentley, and William H. Matchett. Contains "In All These Acts." Collected in *The Hazards of Holiness*.

118. The Commonweal, Vol. LXXVI, No. 12. New York, N.Y., The Commonweal Publishing Co., Inc., June 15, 1962.

Edited by Edward S. Skillin. Contains "God Germed in Raw Granite." Collected in *The Hazards of Holiness*. Anthologized in *A Selection of Contemporary Religious Poetry*.

119. Choice, No. 2. Chicago, Ill., Summer, 1962.

Edited by John Logan. Contains "I Am Long Weaned." Collected in *The Hazards of Holiness.*

120. The Critic; a Catholic Review of Books and the Arts, Vol. XX, No. 6. Chicago, Ill., Thomas More Association, June-July, 1962.

Edited by Paul K. Cuneo. Contains the article, "A Tribute to Robinson Jeffers." Uncollected.

121. The Atlantic Monthly, Vol. CCX, No. 2. Boston, Mass., The Atlantic Monthly Company, August, 1962.

Contains "The Song the Body Dreamed in the Spirit's Mad Behest," from *The Hazards of Holiness.* Anthologized in *Erotic Poetry.*

122. The Critic, Vol. XXI, No. 1. Chicago, Ill., August-September, 1962.

Edited by Paul K. Cuneo. Contains "All the Way to Heaven." Collected in *The Hazards of Holiness.*

123. Ramparts, Vol. I, No. 2. Menlo Park, Calif., The Layman's Press, September, 1962.

Edited by Edward M. Keating. Contains "The Hazards of Holiness: The Beheading of John the Baptist; Judith and Holoferness," and "pages From an Unpublished Autobiography." Also contained is a holograph page, two pictures of the poet, and an article on Brother Antoninus by Harry Stiehl. The poem was collected in *The Hazards of Holiness* as the title poem.

124. Tvgonik Powszechnv, Vol. XVI, No. 32. Krakow, Poland, September 12, 1962.

Contains "Ucieczka na Pustynie" (The Flight in the Desert, from *An Age Insurgent* and *The Crooked Lines of God*), and "Rzez Niewiniatek" (The Massacre of the Holy Innocents, from *The Crooked Lines of God*). Translation by Adriana Zielinskiego.

125. The Commonweal, Vol. LXXVII, No. 5. New York, N.Y., The Commonweal Publishing Co., Inc., October 26, 1962.

Edited by Edward S. Skillin. Contains the article, "Our Modern Sensibility." Uncollected.

126. Encounter, Vol. XIX, No. 6. London, England, December, 1962.

Contains a letter concerning the Spanish movie, *Viridiani.*

127. The Book Club of California Quarterly News Letter, Vol. XXVIII, No. 2. San Francisco, Calif., Spring, 1963.

Pages 31-32 contain a letter from William Everson to Lawrence Clark Powell that is dated March 18, 1947.

128. Way: Catholic Viewpoints, Vol. XIX, No. 6. San Francisco, Calif., Franciscan Fathers of California, Inc., July-August, 1963.

Edited by Ed. Henriques, O. F. M. Contains "Annul in Me My Manhood," from *The Crooked Lines of God.*

129. Approach: A Literary Quarterly, No. 49. Rosemont, Pa., Fall, 1963.

Edited by Albert and Helen Fowler. Contains a comment by Brother Antoninus on a review of *The Hazards of Holiness* by Albert Fowler, and "Dialogue on Holy Violence," a dialogue between Brother Antoninus and Albert Fowler.

130. Way: Catholic Viewpoints, Vol. XIX. San Francisco, Calif., Franciscan Fathers of California, Inc., October, 1963.

Edited by Ed. Henriques, O. F. M. Contains "A Canticle to the Waterbirds," from *The Crooked Lines of God.*

131. Ramparts, Vol. II, No. 3. Menlo Park, Calif., The Layman's Press, Christmas, 1963.

Edited by Edward M. Keating. Contains "The Poet Is Dead" (Collected as *The Poet Is Dead*), and a review of Robinson Jeffer's, *The Beginning and the End.*

132. Season: A Dominican Quarterly of Contemporary Human Problems, Vol. I, No. 4. St. Albert's College, Oakland, Calif., Winter, 1963.

Edited by Jenko Zagar. Contains the article, "Tongs of Jeopardy." Uncollected.

133. Ramparts, Vol. II, No. 5. Menlo Park, Calif., The Layman's Press, Spring, 1964.

Edited by Edward M. Keating. Contains a reprinting of the article, "The Tongs of Jeopardy." Also contained is a drawing of Brother Antoninus by Rita Cooper.

134. Esprit, Vol. VIII, No. 1. Scranton, Pennsylvania, The University of Scranton, Winter, 1964.

Contains a contribution to a symposium on Flannery O'Connor. Uncollected.

135. Dominican, Vol. V, No. 1. Washington, D.C., Dominican House of Studies, Spring, 1965.

Contains the article, "Death Has Pounced," which is an excerpt from an expanded version of "Tongs of Jeopardy."

136. Sketchbook. Collegeville, Minn., St. John's University, Spring, 1965.

Edited by George Roberts. Contains "Rosa Mystica." Uncollected.

169

137. Poets of the Western Scene, edited by Hans A. Hoffman. San Leandro, Calif., Greater West Publishing Co., 1937.

Contains "Do Not Brood for Long," from *These Are the Ravens*.

138. New Directions 9, edited by James Laughlin. Norfolk, Conn., New Directions, 1946.

Clothbound in dust jacket. Contains a "note" and "The Waldport Poems," by William Everson.

139. One Hundred Modern Poems, selected by Selden Rodman. New York, N.Y., Pellegrini & Cudahy, 1949.

Clothbound in dust jacket. Contains "The Raid" by William Everson. Reissued by The New American Library of World Literature, Inc., in March, 1951, as a Mentor Book in paperback.

140. N D 12; New Directions in Prose and Poetry, edited by James Laughlin. Norfolk, Conn., New Directions, 1950.

Clothbound in dust jacket. Contains "Triptych for the Living," by William Everson.

141. Islands of Books, by Lawrence Clark Powell, Los Angeles, Calif., The Ward Ritchie Press, 1951.

Clothbound. Pages 89-92 contain "The Ruin" from *The Masculine Dead*, and "Walls" and "San Joaquin," from *San Joaquin*.

142. Borestone Mountain Poetry Awards 1955 (A Compilation of Original Poetry Published in Magazines of the English-Speaking World in 1954). Stanford, Calif., Stanford University Press, 1955.

Clothbound in dust jacket. Contains "Under a Keeping Spring," by Brother Antoninus.

143. Novum Psalterium PII XII. Los Angeles, Calif., 1955.

Blue morocco. Preliminary pages were printed by Saul and Lillian Marks at the Plantin Press, Los Angeles, California. Bound by Donnelly & Son, Lakeside Press, Chicago, Illinois. Only 48 complete copies were printed and bound by Brother Antoninus as an unfinished folio edition. Foreword by Robert O. Schad. Contains "A Note on the Psalter of Pope Pius XII," by Brother Antoninus. (For a discussion of this book see pp. 135-142.

144. Books in My Baggage: Adventures in Reading and Collecting by Lawrence Clark Powell. Cleveland, The World Publishing Company, 1959.

Clothbound in dust jacket. Page 173 contains the poem, "San Joaquin."

145. HELGON & HETSPORRAR; Poesi fran Beat Generation och San Franciscorenassansen, edited by Reidar Ekner. Stockholm, Sweden, Raben & Sjogren, 1960.

Decorative wrappers. Contains "Ur Askan" [Out of the Ash], and "Upphar i mig min manlighet" [Annul in Me My Manhood], by Brother Antoninus.

146. THE NEW AMERICAN POETRY: 1945-1960, edited by Donald M. Allen. New York, N.Y., Grove Press, Inc., 1960.

Clothbound in dust jacket, and in decorative wrappers [two editions]. Contains "Advent," "A Canticle to the Waterbirds," and "The South Coast," by Brother Antoninus.

147. THE CALIFORNIANS: Writings of Their Past and Present, Vol. II, Edited by Ursule Spier Erickson and Robert Pearsall. San Francisco, Calif., Hesperian House, 1961.

Green cloth over boards in the dust jacket. Contains "Annul in Me My Manhood," "The South Coast," and "Out of the Ash."

148. IN PROGRESS: ALDER GULCH AND OTHER POEMS, by Bill Butler. Berkeley, Calif., Haunted Bookshop & Private Press, 1961.

Printed wrappers. Contains the Introduction by Brother Antoninus.

149. POETRY FESTIVAL (COMMISSIONED POEMS 1962). San Francisco, Calif., Poetry Center, San Francisco State College, 1962.

Decorative wrappers. Poems read at the Poetry Festival held at the San Francisco Museum of Art from June 21 through June 24, 1962. Contains "The Poet Is Dead (A Memorial for Robinson Jeffers)."

150. A SELECTION OF CONTEMPORARY RELIGIOUS POETRY, compiled by Samuel Hazo. Glen Rock, New Jersey, Deus Books/Paulist Press (Paulist Fathers), 1963.

Paperback. (An Original Deus Book.) Contains "God Germed in Raw Granite," by Brother Antoninus.

151. ANTOLOGIA DE LA POESIA NORTEAMERICANA, translated by Jose Coronel Urtecho and Ernesto Cardenal. Madrid, Spain, Aguilar, 1963.

Clothbound in the dust jacket. Contains "Salmo Penitencial" (Penitential Psalm), "Cantico a Las Aves Acuaticas" (Canticle to the Waterbirds), by Brother Antoninus.

152. BEST POEMS OF 1962; Borestone Mountain Poetry Awards 1963. (A compilation of Original Poetry Published in Magazines of the English-Speaking World in 1962.) Fifteenth Annual Issue, Volume XV. Palo Alto, Calif., Pacific Books, Publishers, 1963.

Clothbound in dust jacket. Contains "God Germed in Raw Granite," by Brother Antoninus.

153. EROTIC POETRY: the Lyrics, Ballads, Idyls and Epics of Love—Classical to Contemporary, edited by William Cole. New York, N.Y., Random House, 1963.

Clothbound in dust jacket. Contains "The Song the Body Dreamed in the Spirit's Mad Behest," by Brother Antoninus, and "The Presence," and "March," by William Everson.

154. THE LITTLE PACKAGE, by Lawrence Clark Powell. Cleveland, The World Publishing Company, 1964.

Clothbound in dust jacket. Page 263 contains an excerpt from a letter to Lawrence Clark Powell from Brother Antoninus.

155. MODERN RELIGIOUS POEMS: A Contemporary Anthology, edited by Jacob Trapp. New York, N.Y., Harper & Row, Publishers, 1964.

Clothbound in dust jacket. Contains "Jacob and the Angel," by Brother Antoninus.

156. TODAY's POETS: American and British Poetry Since the 1930's, edited by Chad Walsh. New York, N.Y., Charles Scribner's Sons, 1964.

Contains "August," "The Stranger," "Hospice of the Word," "A Canticle to the Christ in the Holy Eucharist," "A Siege of Silence," "What Birds Were There," "In All These Acts," by Brother Antoninus.

157. SAN FRANCISCO RENAISSANCE: Elleve Moderne Amerikanske Lyrikere, edited by Redigeret af Erik Thygesen. Copenhagen, Denmark, Sirius, 1964.

Wrappers. Contains "En Salme Til Havfuglene" (Canticle to the Waterbirds), by Brother Antoninus. In the introduction Rexroth's statement on Brother Antoninus for the Evergreen Review, Vol. I, No. 2, is translated into Danish.

158. POESIA DEGLI ULTIMI AMERICANI, a cura Fernanda Pivano. Milano, Italy, Le Comete 35, Feltrinelli Editore, November, 1964.

Pictorial wrappers. Contains "Vernichte in Mir Meine Mannheit" (Annul in Me My Manhood), and "Zone des Todes" (Zone of Death), by Brother Antoninus.

159. NUESTRA DECADA: La Cultura Contemporanea a Traves de Mel Textos (Revista de la Universidad de México), Vol. I. Mexico, D.F., Universidad Nacional Autonoma de Mexico, 1964.

Black cloth over boards. Contains "Salmo Penitenciario," and "Cántico de las aves acuáticas."

160. THE TREE AND THE MASTER: an Anthology of Literature on the Cross of Christ, edited by Sister Mary Immaculate. New York, N.Y., Random House, 1965.

Clothbound in dust jacket. Contains "The Making of the Cross," by Brother Antoninus.

161. STUDYING POETRY: a Critical Anthology of English and American Poems, edited by Karl Kroeber and John O. Lyons. New York, N.Y., Harper & Row, Publishers, 1965.

Clothbound. Contains "Canticle to the Waterbirds," by Brother Antoninus.

162. SECOND READING: selections from the *Quarterly News Letter* 1933-1963, compiled by Oscar Lewis. San Francisco, Calif., The Book Club of California, 1965.

Clothbound. 425 copies only. Contains "Latter-day Handpress," by William Everson, and a fold-out reproduction of The Equinox Press broadside.

163. 1966 PEACE CALENDAR & APPOINTMENT BOOK: Poems of War Resistance. New York, N.Y., War Registers League, 1966.

Pictorial wrappers, spiral bound. Contains "The Unkillable Knowledge (Spring 1941)," from the *War Elegies* books, by William Everson.

164. HARVARD ADVOCATE CENTENNIAL ANTHOLOGY, edited by Jonathan D. Culler. Cambridge, Mass., Schenkman Publishing Co., Inc., 1966.

Clothbound in dust jacket. Contains the interview, "A Conversation with Brother Antoninus," which is reprinted in abridgment from The Harvard Advocate. The drawing of Brother Antoninus is by Tony Pore. -

PHONOGRAPH RECORDINGS

165. WILLIAM EVERSON ALBUM. Audition [records], Berkeley, Calif. 1947.

This was not a pressing; each record was cut individually to order.

166. SAN FRANCISCO POETS. Evergreen Records, Lp, No. EVR-1, New York, 1957.

Contains booklet of poems recorded and photos of the poets. (Now distributed by Hanover Records, New York.) Brother Antoninus reads two of his poems: "The South Coast," and "Out of the Ash."

167. THE TONGS OF JEOPARDY (a Meditation on the Death of President Kennedy), by Brother Antoninus. Memorare Recordings, Inc., Lp, CH 103, Los Angeles, Calif., 1964.

CRITICISM

SAN JOAQUIN, by William Everson. Los Angeles, Calif., The Ward Ritchie Press, June, 1939.

Foreword by Lawrence Clark Powell.

Poetry: A Magazine of Verse, Vol. LVI, No. 4. Chicago, Ill., Poetry, July, 1940.

Edited by George Dillon. Pages 220-222 contain "Four Poets," by Jean Prussing, which includes a review of San Joaquin.

The New Republic, Vol. 109, No. 5. New York, N.Y., August 2, 1943.

Pages 148-150 contain "Poetry for All Tastes," by David Dachies, which contains a review of The Masculine Dead, and X War Elegies.

Poetry: A Magazine of Verse, Vol. LXIII, No. 1. Chicago, Ill., Poetry, October, 1943.

Edited by George Dillon. Pages 52-55 contain "Magic and Melancholy," by Nelson Algren, a review of The Masculine Dead and X War Elegies.

The Compass, Vol. I, No. 6. West Compton, N.H., Spring, 1944.

Pages 38-39 contain a review of X War Elegies by Kenneth Bache.

The Compass, Vol. II, Nos. 1 & 2. West Compton, N.H., Summer & Fall, 1944.

Edited by Martin Ponch. Page 40 contains a review of The Waldport Poems by Ruth Suckow.

The San Francisco Chronicle, January 21, 1945.

Contains a review of War Elegies.

Poetry: A Magazine of Verse, Vol. LXV, No. 5. Chicago, Ill., Poetry, February, 1945.

Edited by Peter DeVries and Marion Strobel. Pages 281-282 contain "Minority Report" by Donald F. Drummon, a review of War Elegies.

Accent: A Quarterly of New Literature. Urbana, Illinois, Accent, Spring, 1945.

Edited by Kerker Quinn, Charles Shattuck, and Allan Holaday. Pages 190-191 contain a review of War Elegies and Waldport Poems by J. F. Powers.

174

Poetry: A Magazine of Verse, Vol. LXVI, No. 5. Chicago, Ill., Poetry, August, 1945.

Edited by Peter DeVries and Marion Strobel. Pages 284-289 contain "Conscience: Personal, Political, Philosophical" by Mona Van Duyn, a review of *War Elegies*.

Circle, No. 5, Berkeley, Calif. 1945.

Edited by George Leite. Contains a review of *War Elegies* by George Thurston [pseudonym of George Leite].

Poetry: A Magazine of Verse, Vol. LXVIII, No. 4. Chicago, Ill., Poetry, July, 1946

Edited by George Dillon, Marion Strobel, Margedant Peters, and John Frederick Nims. Pages 227-231 contain "Goodness, Substance, Eloquence," by Harvey Curtis Webster, which contains a review of *Poems: MCMXLII*.

Chicago Tribune, Book Section, July 7, 1946.

Page 1 contains "Freshness (Plus Brashness) in New Directions Book," a review of *New Directions IX*, which contains a review of "The Waldport Poems," by Paul Engle.

Poetry: A Magazine of Verse, Vol. LXVIII, No. 6. Chicago, Ill., Poetry, September, 1946.

Edited by George Dillon, Marion Stroble, Margedant Peters, and John Frederick Nims. Pages 352-355 contain "The Newest Is Clarity," a review of *New Directions IX*, which contains a review of "The Waldport Poems" by Ruth Lechlitner.

Now, No. 7. London, England, Autumn, 1946.

Edited by George Woodstock. Pages 59-65 contain the epistolary article by Kenneth Rexroth, "Letter from America."

The Sewanee Review, Vol. LIV, No. 4. Sewanee, Tenn., The University of the South, October-December, 1946.

Edited by S. E. Palmer. Pages 699-716 contain "Poetry Chronicle," a review of *Poems: MCMXLII*, by Vivienne Koch.

Horizon, Vol. XVI, Nos. 93-94. London, England, October, 1947.

Edited by Cyril Connelly. Pages 118-123 contain the epistolary article by Philip Lamantia, "Letter from San Francisco." Brother Antoninus is given prominent mention.

The Tiger's Eye, Vol. I, No. 4. New York, N.Y., June, 1948.

Page 109 contains "The Poetry Bulletin," a review of *The Residual Years*.

California Library Bulletin, Vol. IX, No. 4. Los Angeles, Calif., California Library Association, June, 1948.

Edited by Neal Harlow. Pages 119-122 contain "San Joaquin Vision," by Lawrence Clark Powell.

San Quentin News. San Quentin, Calif., June 11, 1948.

Contains "Poet Decries Wars Meaning," a review of *War Elegies*, by H., G. S.

The Los Angeles Times, June 13, 1948.

Contains "Youthful Coast Poet Tries to Bridge Gap," a review of *The Residual Years*.

The Providence Journal, Providence, R.I., June 13, 1948.

Contains a review of *The Residual Years*, by Winifried Townley Scott.

The Partisan Review, Vol. XV, No. 8. New York, N.Y., Added Enterprises, August, 1948.

Edited by William Phillips, and Philip Rahv. Pages 924-931 contain "Some Uses and Abuses of Feeling" by Leslie Fiedler, which contains a review of *The Residual Years*.

The San Francisco Chronicle, This World, November 7, 1948.

Page 9 contains "The New Poetry," a review of *The Residual Years*, by Thomas Hornsby Ferrill.

The Occident, Berkeley, Calif., University of California at Berkeley, Fall, 1948.

Pages 41-43 contain "Two Sides of a Continent" by Byram Dans Sedgewick, which contains a review of *The Residual Years*.

The Saturday Review, Vol. XXXI, No. 47. New York, N.Y., Saturday Review Association, Inc., November 20, 1948.

Page 32 contains the article "Subjective Weighing and Writhing," by Dudley Fitts, which contains a review of *The Residual Years*.

The New Mexico Quarterly Review, Vol. XVIII, No. 4. Albuquerque, New Mexico, University of New Mexico, Winter, 1948.

Page 465 contains a review of *The Residual Years* by Deane Mowrer.

The Pacific Spectator, Vol. IV, No. 3. Palo Alto, Calif., Stanford University, Summer, 1950.

Pages 290-305 contain "Some Recent Pacific Coast Poetry," by Thomas Parkinson, which contains a review of *The Residual Years*.

The Western Review, Vol. XV, No. 1. Autumn, 1950.

Pages 68-73 contain "From Aridity to Affirmation," by George Brandon Saul, which contains a review of *The Residual Years*.

Rough Weather, No. 1. Los Angeles, Calif., Spring, 1951.

Edited by San Novit. Page 27 contains a review of "A Privacy of Speech."

Western Printer & Lithographer. Los Angeles, Calif., July, 1951.

Edited by Roby Wentz. Page 28 contains an article on Brother Antoninus' Seraphim Press.

Islands of Books, by Lawrence Clark Powell. Los Angeles, Calif., The Ward Ritchie Press, 1951.

Clothbound. Pages 89-92 concern William Everson.

The Catholic Worker, Vol. XVIII, No. 18. New York, N.Y., The Catholic Worker, February, 1953.

Edited by Dorothy Day. Contains the article "Life of Prayer," by Dorothy Day.

Printing & Graphic Arts, Vol. I, No. 1. Lunenburg, Vermont, The Stinehour Press, February, 1953.

Edited by Rollo G. Silver. Page 14 contains a paragraph on Brother Antoninus concerning the printing of the *Psalter*.

The Nation, Vol. CLXXXIV, No. 8. New York, N.Y., Nation Associates, Inc., February 23, 1957.

Edited by Carey McWilliams. Pages 159-162 contain "San Francisco's Mature Bohemians," by Kenneth Rexroth. Brother Antoninus is given significant mention.

Evergreen Review, Vol. I, No. 2. New York, N.Y., Grove Press, Inc., 1957.

Edited by Barney Rosset and Donald Allen. Pages 5-14 contain the article "San Francisco Letter," by Kenneth Rexroth. Brother Antoninus is given prominent mention.

The Bay Window, Vol. I, No. 1. San Francisco, Calif., August 21, 1957.

Edited by Cleveland E. Twitchell. Contains the article "Grove Press and the Evergreen Review," by Harry Stiehl.

Life, Vol. 43, No. 11. Chicago, Ill., Time, Inc., September 9, 1957.

Pages 105-109 contain the article "Big Day for Bards at Bay."

The Saturday Review, Vol. XL, No. 47. New York, N.Y., Saturday Review, Inc., November 23, 1957.

Page 32 contains the article "Writers as Readers of Poetry," by John Ciardi, which includes a review of *San Francisco Poets* (Evergreen Records).

The San Francisco Bay Window, Vol. 2, No. 1. San Francisco, Calif., April 30, 1958.

Edited by Cleveland E. Twitchell. Page 6 contains the article "S. F. Renaissance: The First Phase," by Harry Stiehl.

Library Journal, Vol. 83, No. 12. New York, N.Y., R. R. Bowker Co., June 15, 1958.

Edited by Lee Ash. Pages 1850-1854 contain the article "California's Young Writers, Angry and Otherwise," by Basil Ross. Brother Antoninus is given significant mention and is pictured in a photo by Harry Redl.

The San Francisco Bay Window, San Francisco, Calif., October 29, 1958.

Page 6 contains "New Work by Brother Antoninus," an article by Harry Stiehl announcing the publication of the broadside *At the Edge*.

Reflections, Vol. 8, No. 1. Oakland, Calif., College of the Holy Names, 1958.

Edited by Kathleen Kemp. Page 11 contains "American Catholic Poetry, 1930-1958," by Harry Stiehl.

Fresco: the University of Detroit Quarterly, Vol. IX, No. 2. Detroit, Michigan, Winter, 1958.

Edited by Steve Eisner. Pages 4-10 contain the article, "Antoninus, Thrihedral Poet," by Jerome Mazzaro.

Time Magazine, Vol. LXXIII, No. 21. Chicago, Ill., Time Inc., May 25, 1959.

Pages 58, 60 contain the article "The Beat Friar." Also contained is a photograph of Brother Antoninus.

Jubilee: A Magazine of the Church and Her People, Vol. VII, No. 4. New York, N.Y., A. M. D. G. Publishing Co., Inc., August, 1959.

Edited by Edward Rice. Pages 42-45 contain a picture article on Brother Antoninus.

The Varsity News, University of Detroit, February 23, 1960.

Page 1 contains "Antoninus Poetry to Be Considered for Pulitzer Prize," a feature article with photograph, on the occasion of *The Crooked Lines of God* being nominated for the Pulitzer Prize. The photo is by Mark Lansburgh and was taken at St. Albert's College in Oakland, California, in 1956, and not, as the caption claims, on the poet's last visit to the Detroit campus.

The Commonweal, Vol. LXXI, No. 24. New York, N.Y., The Commonweal Publishing Co., Inc., March 11, 1960.

Edited by Edward S. Skillin. Page 656 contains "Poetry of Conversion and the Religious Life," a review of *The Crooked Lines of God*, by Rosemary F. Deen.

The New York Times Book Review. March 27, 1960.

Page 10 contains "A Struggle to Prepare for Vision," a review of *The Crooked Lines of God*, by Kenneth Rexroth.

Los Angeles Herald & Express. April 25, 1960.

Page A-12 contains a review of *The Crooked Lines of God*, by Thomas P. McDonnell.

The Critic: A Catholic Review of Books and the Arts, Vol. XVIII, No. 5. Chicago, Ill., Thomas More Association, April-May, 1960.

Edited by Paul K. Cuneo. Pages 28-29 contain a review of *The Crooked Lines of God*, by Thomas P. McDonnell. A photograph of Brother Antoninus appears on page 28.

Big Table, Vol. I, No. 4. Chicago, Ill., Big Table, Inc., 1960.

Edited by Paul Carroll. Pages 128-132 contain "Writing for the Ear," by Paul Blackburn, a review of *San Francisco Poets* (Hanover Records).

The New Mexico Quarterly Review, Vol. XXX, No. 2. Albuquerque, New Mexico, University of New Mexico, Summer, 1960.

Pages 119-200 contain a review of *The Crooked Lines of God*, by Ralph J. Mills.

Spirit: A Magazine of Poetry, Vol. XXVII, No. 3. New York, N.Y., July, 1960.

Pages 81-84 contain "Oratorio" by James Edward Tobin, which contains a review of *The Crooked Lines of God*.

Sewanee Review. Sewanee, Tenn., University of the South, Autumn, 1960.

Contains "The Suspect in Poetry," a review by James Dickey of *The Crooked Lines of God*.

Voices: A Journal of Poetry, No. 173. September-December, 1960.

Pages 32-35 contain "Hitting It Lucky" by Lewis Turco, which contains a review of *The Crooked Lines of God*.

The Catholic Northwest Progress. Seattle, Washington, Friday, May 26, 1961.

Page 5 contains a review of *The Crooked Lines of God*, by John J. Eckhart.

Spirit: A Magazine of Poetry, Vol. XXVIII, No. 2. New York, N.Y., May, 1961.

Pages 54-60 contain "The Poetry of Brother Antoninus," by Thomas P. McDonnell.

Assays, by Kenneth Rexroth. New York, N.Y., New Directions, 1961.

Pages 230-231 contain a review of *The Crooked Lines of God*.

Poetry Dial, Vol. I, No. 2. Spring, 1961.

Pages 44-45 contain a review of *The Crooked Lines of God*, Dennis Schmitz.

Catherine Wheel. St. Paul, Minn., College of St. Catherine, November 1, 1961.

Contains articles on Brother Antoninus by Mary Ellen Blacik, and Kathy Neils.

Approach: A Literary Quarterly, No. 38. Rosemont, Pa., Winter, 1961.

Pages 40-41 contain "The Precise Words," by Helen Fowler, a review of *The Crooked Lines of God*.

Poetry, Vol. 99, No. 4. Chicago, Ill., Poetry, January, 1962.

Edited by Henry Rago. Pages 253-258 contain the article "Two Religious Poets," by John Engels, which contains a review of *The Crooked Lines of God*.

The New York Times Book Review, Vol. LXVII, No. 36. September 9, 1962.

Page 4 contains "Pleasure and Anguish" by M. L. Rosenthal, which contains a review of *The Hazards of Holiness*, and pages 5, 34 contain "Between Verses: Report on a West Coast Poetry Festival," by Jack Gilbert.

The Press Democrat. San Jose, Calif., September 9, 1962.

Contains "Work of Poetry, an Act of Relief," a review of *The Hazards of Holiness*.

Catholic Reporter. Kansas City, Mo., September 21, 1962.

Contains a review of *The Hazards of Holiness*, by Herbert A. Kenny.

The Pilot. Boston, Mass., September 22, 1962.

Contains "Bleeding Trophies," a review of *The Hazards of Holiness*, by Joseph McLellan.

Long Island Catholic. Rockville Center, N.Y., October 18, 1962.

Contains "Brown Habit Among Beards," a review of *The Hazards of Holiness*, by J. G. M.

The Commonweal, Vol. LXXVII, No. 4. Norwalk, Conn., The Commonweal Publishing Co., Inc., October 19, 1962.

Pages 100-101 contain "Antoninus' Night," a review by Janet Fiscalini of *The Hazards of Holiness.*

Jubilee: A Magazine of the Church and Her People, Vol. 10, No. 7. New York, N.Y., A. M. D. G. Publishing Co., November, 1962.

Pages 54-55 contain a review of *The Hazards of Holiness,* by Peter Levi, S.J.

Library Journal, Vol. 87, No. 19. Philadelphia, Pa., R. R. Bowker Co., November 1, 1962.

Edited by Margaret E. Cooley. Page 4025 contains a review of *The Hazards of Holiness,* by Herbert Burke.

Peninsula Living. Palo Alto, Calif., November 4, 1962.

Contains a review of *The Hazards of Holiness,* by Clyde Collard.

The New York Times Book Review. December 2, 1962.

Page 7 contains a review of *The Hazards of Holiness* by Thomas Lask.

Golden Gater, San Francisco State College, Tuesday, December 4, 1962.

Contains "Jeffers 'Memorial' Features Brother Antoninus Miksak."

The San Francisco Examiner, December 16, 1962.

Section I, page 22 contains an interview with Brother Antoninus conducted by Lisa Hobbs.

San Francisco Sunday Chronicle, This World, December 23, 1962.

Pages 21-22 contain the article "The Poets Speak From a Deep Personal Point of View," which contains a review of *The Hazards of Holiness.*

The Benedictine Review, Vol. XVIII, No. 1. Collegeville, Minn., St. John's University, January, 1963.

Pages 87-88 contain a review of *The Hazards of Holiness,* by O.S.B. Schuster.

Way: Catholic Viewpoints, Vol. XIX, No. 1. San Francisco, Calif., Franciscan Fathers of California, Inc., January- February, 1963.

Edited by Henriques, O.F.M. Pages 46-51 contain the article "Brother Antoninus," by A. V. Krebs, Jr.

The Catholic Book Reporter, March, 1963.

Page 45 contains a review of *The Hazards of Holiness,* by Phillip Hanley, S.J.

University of Nevada Sagebrush. Reno, Nevada, March 26, 1963.

Page 3 contains "Religious Poets Are Few Today," a review of *The Hazards of Holiness*, by Tremallo, F. G.

The Commonweal, Vol. LXXVIII, No. 1. New York, N.Y., The Commonweal Publishing Co., Inc., March 29, 1963.

Edited by Edward S. Skillin. Pages 13-14 contain the article "Poet From the West (Evenings with Brother Antoninus)," by Thomas P. McDonnell.

The Catholic World. New York, N.Y., April 1963.

Pages 61, 63 contain a review of *The Hazards of Holiness*, by Joseph Tusiani.

Poetry, Vol. 102, No. 1. Chicago, Ill., Poetry, April, 1963.

Edited by Henry Rago. Pages 42-48 contain " 'Think What's Got Away . . .' ," by Robert Creeley, which contains a review of *The Hazards of Holiness*.

Dominicana, Vol. 48, No. 1. Washington, D.C., Dominicana House of Studies, Spring, 1963.

Pages 33-53 contain "Brother Antoninus: A Symposium," by Brendan Cavanaugh, O.P., Alfred Camillus Murphy, O. P., and Joseph Albert Doshner, O.P. Page 32 contains a grease-pencil sketch of Brother Antoninus by "Myers."

The Critic: A Catholic Review of Books and the Arts, Vol. XVIII, No. 5. Chicago, Ill., Thomas More Association, April-May, 1963.

Pages 85-86 contain a review of *The Hazards of Holiness*, by John Logan.

The Catholic Worker, Vol. XXIX, No. 10. New York, N.Y., The Catholic Worker, May 1, 1963.

Page 5 contains a review of *The Hazards of Holiness*, by Jean Forest.

The Harvard Advocate, Vol. XCVII, No. 3. Cambridge, Mass., Spring-Summer, 1963.

Pages 32-46 contain a printed transcription of a tape-recorded interview with Brother Antoninus.

The San Francisco Examiner, May 12, 1963.

Contains "Two Poets and a Struggle," which contains a review of *The Hazards of Holiness*.

The Minnesota Review, Vol. III, No. 4. Minneapolis, Minn., Summer, 1963.

Pages 473-491 contains "James Dickey and Other Good Poets," by Jean Forest, which contains a review of *The Hazards of Holiness*.

Approach: A Literary Quarterly, No. 49. Rosemont, Pa., Fall, 1963.

Pages 40-44 contain a review of *The Hazards of Holiness*, by Albert Fowler.

The Atlantic Monthly, Vol. CCXII, No. 6. Boston, Mass., December, 1963.

Pages 82-85 contain a review of *The Hazards of Holiness*, by Peter Davison.

The Suspect in Poetry, by James Dickey. Madison, Minn., The Sixties Press, 1964.

Clothbound in dust jacket and in wrappers [two editions]. Pages 97-99 contain the sub-chapter, "Brother Antoninus."

Contemporary American Poetry, by Ralph J. Mills, Jr. New York, N.Y., Random House, 1965.

Wrappers. Contains Chapter V,"Brother Antoninus (William Everson)."

Echoings Magazine, Vol. 12. Philadelphia, Pa., William T. Cooke Publishing, Inc., February, 1966.

Pages 44-45 contain the article "Poet of the Direct Statement," by Eileen M. Regan.

SINGLE SOURCE: The Early Poems of William Everson [1934-1940]. Berkeley, Calif., Oyez, April, 1966.

Introduction by Robert Duncan.